Organic

CHRISTIAN

LIFE

Kenneth E. Purcell

Organic Christian Life

Trilogy Christian Publishers A Wholly Owned Subsidiary of Trinity Broadcasting Network

2442 Michelle Drive Tustin, CA 92780

Manufactured in the United States of America

10 9 8 7 6 5 4 3 2 1

Library of Congress Cataloging-in-Publication Data is available.

ISBN: 978-1-63769-264-6

E-ISBN: 978-1-63769-265-3

Dedication

Knowledge and wisdom are distinct from each other. One can have knowledge but lack wisdom. One can have wisdom but have very little education. This book is dedicated to the use and service of both. It is my hope that the reader will gain knowledge and wisdom from digesting the content found in these pages.

Acknowledgments

June Brassard, who recently passed away at age 91, was the key person who introduced me into a life of authentic faith. Her faith in God and persistent prayers for my mom and myself changed the trajectory of my life. The support from my wife and our two sons have been of incalculable value. A special thanks to Janice Gribben for her constant encouragement.

Contents

Introduction

Hello, my name is Ken. I am a Christian. Not much of an introduction, I know. When I tell someone I am a Christian, the perception of the listener may be like this: *Okay, so you are not a Muslim, atheist, Hindu, Jew, or any other category of religious adherent.* "I am a Christian" has lost the impact it once had. The word *Christ* means "anointed one."

In Luke 4:18, Jesus said, *"The Spirit of the Lord is upon me, because he hath anointed me to preach the gospel to the poor; he hath sent me to heal the broken hearted, to preach deliverance to the captives, and recovering of sight to the blind, to set at liberty them that are bruised"* (KJV).

In Acts 10:38, we are told *"how God anointed Jesus of Nazareth with the Holy Spirit and power, and how he went around doing good and healing all who were under the power of the devil, because God was with him"* (NIV).

To be a Christian means to represent the One who is anointed: Jesus.

1

How I Met the Anointed One

I was raised as a Roman Catholic. I learned stories from the Bible. I learned about Jesus and how He was crucified for our sins. I learned that Jesus rose from the dead and ascended to heaven. But that was about all I knew. I did not know this Jesus any more than I knew some movie star. I began to feel sick and experienced unusual symptoms around the age of sixteen. I no longer had the energy I once had. I felt so weak all the time. It was way more than just being tired. Doctors were not sure what I had, because nothing in my lab work indicated cancer or any other serious disease.

I attended a healing service conducted by a Catholic priest named Ralph DiOrio. It was unlike any Catholic mass I had ever attended. There was something very different happening there. There was a tangible spiritual presence in the building. It was Jesus visiting the building. Words alone cannot describe the way that felt.

I would soon encounter the very same presence in my

room. The Anointed One would soon enter my room, just as He did in that building. That was the day Jesus came to visit. I did not see Him in physical form, but just like Mary at the tomb (John 20:16), when He called my name, I recognized Him instantly and instinctively. His voice was warm and loving. When He spoke, the atmosphere was permeated with peace. His voice seemed to fill the room, and it sounded like many waters (Ezekiel 43:2) flowing in and out of my earthly surroundings. There was no denying that something supernatural happened in those moments. Heaven kissed earth when the Anointed One appeared. God was no longer some faraway being. He was now a very real part of me. His Spirit and mine joined as one.

To whom God would make known what is the riches of the glory of this mystery among the Gentiles; which is Christ in you, the hope of glory.

—Colossians 1:27 KJV

I like to think of it this way: The Anointed One lives in me! This is where our organic Christian life begins. We do not represent a religion. We represent a Person: the Anointed One, Jesus. Pure and simple, this is who He is.

The very same anointing that healed thousands of people then, also began to effect a healing in me. The energy I once had began to infuse my body. The healing was felt immediately, and it became more and more evident over time.

Something about that anointing caused an overflow in my

life. I wanted others to feel the way I felt. I looked at others through eyes of love and compassion. I would offer to pray for people right on the spot. Many times, the people I prayed for felt this same anointing. It manifested in various ways. Sometimes it felt like a warm blanket; sometimes it felt like warmth from the inside; sometimes it felt like waves of love or waves of peace.

The end result was a sense of being close to God and some kind of healing. In John 7:38, Jesus said, *"He who believes in Me, as the Scripture said, 'From his innermost being will flow rivers of living water'"* (NASB). I had heard this quoted from the Bible before, but now I was experiencing the very words of Jesus being lived out through me.

This is eternal life, that they may know You, the only true God, and Jesus Christ whom You have sent.
—John 17:3 NASB

The Gospel is actually very simple: It is to know God, to really know *who* He is. Think of someone you know very well. Most, if not all, of what you learned about this person came by experiencing life together. The Greek word "know" in the above reference is *ginosko*: It means to know by experience or firsthand acquaintance. It is used in Luke 1:34, for example, when Mary, who was a virgin, said she did not *know* a man. To know God would indicate a level of deep intimacy. The way this often looks is by talking to God throughout the day and night. Imagine you have an invisible partner with you as you go through your daily routine. Take time to pause once in a while and listen for the gentle voice inside of you as He works with you. No one does this perfectly, so allow yourself to grow into knowing God.

2

Naturally

Why do birds chirp? Why do dogs bark? It is in their nature. They do it naturally. Picture a turtle. A turtle is slow by nature. I can recall a cartoon from my youth where a rocket was strapped to the turtle in order to help it win the proverbial race against the rabbit. Some may label this turtle as speedy, yet that is not who he is nor what he is like. Many people from all generations have placed labels on God that are not true to His nature.

"Getting to Know You" is a showtune from the 1951 musical *The King and I* by Rodgers and Hammerstein. The song has recently been used by ad agencies to promote DNA testing sites. The first two lines are: "Getting to know you, getting to know *all* about you..." The question we need to ask ourselves is, Are we getting to know God? I like to think of the story of Adam and Eve. I picture them walking in the garden. What did they talk about? What did they learn? How did they talk to God? What was the conversation like? What was their perception of God? They did not have a Bible as we do today. So, how did they get to know God? They must have had personal interactions and conversations just as we would with someone close to us. Ahh, getting to know You, the God of all creation. How? Naturally. Relational learning is far superior to learning by reading about someone. Sad to say, but some Christians would be absolutely lost if they had no access to a Bible. The Bible is an integral part of growing in our faith, yet Jesus made it so clear that life itself is discovered in knowing God. Getting to know all about who He is and what He is like is a process that takes time. The Bible can be very helpful in this process, but if it is not understood properly in the framework of the entirety of the culture in which it was written, it may cause our view of God to be distorted and not so clear. I believe to follow Jesus as our Savior, Redeemer, and the Shepherd of our soul will bring clarity to our faith.

The Garden of Eden must have been an absolute wonder for Adam and Eve to behold. It is certainly possible that they learned much about the very nature of God by observing the wonderful world of nature around them. Romans 1:20 tells us, *"For since the creation of the world God's invisible qualities—his eternal power and divine nature—have been clearly seen, being understood from what has been made, so that people are without excuse"* (NIV).

What qualities can be ascribed to God by observing

creation? He is extremely creative! He has superior intelligence. He is absolutely the most talented artist ever! He is amazing at mechanical engineering. He is the most forward-thinking Person who ever existed! For example, just the seed principle alone self-perpetuates life, when a seed is combined with water, air, and sunlight. The foresight of all those elements working together is beyond our imagination. The complexity of all life working together in synchronization is astonishing!

The beauty of creation is beyond description. If all we knew was our observation of creation, we could tell that God was and is the Giver of life. We would see Him as someone who takes tender care of what He gives life to. We would see Him as someone who loves deeply, so deeply that every detail is known and planned so as to ensure the best outcome if left to a natural course. *Loving, caring, concerned, tender, comforting, joyful, peaceful, delightful, awesome, incredible, relational, involved,* and such are the words we would use to describe our view of God. It is true that perspective matters. This could be the way Adam and Eve viewed God. The influence of religious thought has obscured such a pristine view. Take time to observe nature as well as the world around you. Take time to notice what you notice. Be present in the moment. Do you see God as loving or angry? Do you see

Him as distant and aloof or as close as your breath and interested in engagement with you?

3

God Is: _____

Love

Whoever who does not love does not know God, because God is love.

—1 John 4:8 NIV

He who is destitute of love has never had any knowledge of God; because God is love.

—WEYMOUTH

We have come to know and have believed the love which God has for us. God is love, and the one who abides in love abides in God, and God abides in him.

—1 John 4:16 NASB

As for us, we have known experientially the love which God has in our case, and have that knowledge at present, and we have believed and at present maintain that attitude. God is, as to his nature, love, and he who dwells in the aforementioned love in God is dwelling, and God in him is dwelling.

—WUEST

The very nature of God is love. His nature is not hatred. The Wuest translation brings out the present tense, as well as the fact that this love from God is not learned, but rather experienced. When we experience the love that flows from God, He dwells in us and we dwell in Him. The main message coming from the Christian Church has largely been to bring people to church so they can get saved and thereby go to heaven when they die. In other words, the goal has been for us to someday dwell in heaven. The real message of the Gospel is for heaven to dwell in us while we are here on earth. The natural consequence of having heaven inside you (Christ in you) would be access to heaven upon death.

Now you are no longer strangers to God and foreigners to heaven, but you are members of God's very own family, citizens of God's country, and you belong in God's household with every other Christian.

—Ephesians 2:19 TLB

We are citizens of heaven and earth. We have a dual citizenship!

A traditional reading at a wedding ceremony is from 1 Corinthians 13, commonly known as the love chapter. You may recognize the words: Love is patient, love is kind, etc. We know that God is love, therefore I sometimes use the words *God* and *love* interchangeably. First Corinthians 13:4–7 would then read this way: "*God is patient, God is kind. He does not envy, He does not boast, He is not proud.*

He does not dishonor others, He is not self-seeking, He is not easily angered, He keeps no record of wrongs. He does not delight in evil, but rejoices with the truth. God always protects, always trusts, always hopes, always perseveres" (NIV).

I really like the way J.B. Phillips translates verses 7 and 8: *"Love knows no limit to its endurance, no end to its trust, no fading of its hope; it can outlast anything. It is, in fact, the one thing that still stands when all else has fallen."*

Is this the way you have come to see God? If not, then consider adjusting your perspective.

Light

This then is the message which we have heard of him, and declare unto you, that God is light, and in him is no darkness at all.

—1 John 1:5 KJV

The movie *Star Wars* was playing in theaters in 1977. It portrayed the epic battle between good and evil, light and darkness. The Jedi harness the light side of the force, while the Sith harness the dark side of the force. The character known as Anakin was once a student of the light, but he was seduced over to the dark side and became Darth Vader.

Unlike people, God cannot be drawn to the dark side. In fact, there is absolutely no darkness in Him at all. He does not participate in darkness, for He is light. This is His nature: light. People from all cultures often attribute to God the characteristics of darkness, such as anger, judgment, wrath, murder, tragedies, and natural disasters. Christians sometimes fall into this misguided way of viewing God, as well. The Bible does mention judgment and wrath; however, if that is the lens we look through, we might be guilty of making false accusations.

Full of Mercy

O give thanks unto the LORD; for he is good and his mercy endureth forever.

—1 Chronicles 16:34 KJV

Know that the LORD, He is God: it is He who has made us, and not we ourselves; we are His people and the sheep of His pasture. For the LORD is good; His mercy is everlasting; and His truth endures to all generations.

—Psalm 100:3, 5 NKJV

Mercy triumphs over judgment.

—James 2:13 NASB

These three passages from the Bible are either true or false. I have chosen to believe these verses perfectly reflect the nature of God. There are many views that differ from this one. Some have made this complicated. A decisive decision needs to be made. Is this the nature of God? Yes or no. Make it a settled issue. This will be of tremendous help as we nav-

22

igate through life. How we view God will directly affect the way we represent God to others.

Sad to say, God has often been misrepresented by those who claim to know Him. Think about how we define ourselves. I am not defined by my job or my looks or any other of my life circumstances. I am defined by who I am. My character and the way I conduct myself defines me better than the current moment I navigate. Likewise, God should not be defined by temporary life situations. God should be defined by His nature or character—in other words, who He is and always will be. He is love. He is light. He is full of mercy.

4

Jesus Is: _____

The One Who Removes All Sin

The next day John saw Jesus coming toward him, and said, "Behold! The Lamb of God who takes away the sin of the world!"

—John 1:29 NKJV

What is remarkable about this statement? There is no indication that Jesus had healed anyone, declared forgiveness for anyone, performed miracles, or died on a cross at the time when John made this public statement. John prophesied the identity of Jesus, the Lamb of God, as well as future events that would soon take place and change history.

We need to break down this statement and discover the treasures within it. Jesus takes away the sins of the world. What is sin, exactly? The Bible was not written in English; therefore, it is helpful to look at the Greek and Hebrew root words. According to *Strong's Concordance*, the word *sin* means "to miss the mark; to fail."

The consensus has been that this is in reference to archery. The arrow must hit the bull's-eye within the target. Sin is a failure to hit the bull's-eye. In other words, sin is to miss the mark or to fall short. I like to frame this in this way: Sin is any area where we miss the mark, whether in thought, word, and deed. No one has been perfectly on target all the time, except Jesus. John said that Jesus came to take away the sins of the world. The words *take away* come from the Greek word *Airo*. It means to take upon one's self and carry what has been raised up; to raise up and bear away; to remove; to take away from another. This is what Jesus did! He literally removed sin! From who? Only from those who believe? Nay, nay. From the world! From everyone who has ever lived.

Forgiveness is the absolute best gift anyone can give and receive. It is simple, and it has the ability to change anyone and everything. We sometimes make it complex by adding to this very simple formula.

Upstate New York, where I live and work, had a very popular family bakery. They made fresh Italian bread, rolls, and pizza dough, and they were the best at it! It was a simple recipe. They used flour, water, salt, and yeast. Nothing else was added. This locally baked bread was delivered to the stores the same day it was baked. It would not last long, because there were no preservatives or additives, but that was no problem for it was easy to consume a loaf in two days. It was simply irresistible. When the last family member of that family-owned business passed away, the bakery still operated, but it soon began to make changes. They started adding other ingredients. They made the loaves smaller and increased the price. It did not take long before they lost their customers and sales. They eventually went out of business. This bakery left its first love, and the culture it had once impacted lost the desire for the product. The lesson here is to keep it pure and simple. The good news of the Gospel of Jesus is absolute forgiveness, with nothing else added.

The apostle Paul described this absolute forgiveness this way in 2 Corinthians 5:21: "*He made Him who knew no sin to be sin on our behalf, so that we might become the righteousness of God in Him*" (NASB). This is commonly known as the great exchange. The Lamb of God—Jesus—took away our sins, and then He went beyond that by imputing righteousness to us provided we are in Jesus. We therefore conclude that God does not see us for what we have done, but He sees us for what Jesus did. The forgiveness is not earned; neither is righteousness earned. There is a tendency in Christian culture to focus on the do's and the don'ts. Good behavior is always the right thing to do. However, bad behavior cannot undo what Jesus has already done. He has already taken the sin away as it pertains to being alienated from God.

Our sin does have consequences in this life. We cannot unscramble eggs once they are scrambled; therefore we should do our absolute best not to sin. However, when we miss the mark, we can have confidence that our weaknesses will not separate us from God. That would be unjust in the light of how Jesus became sin for us.

The Exact Image of God

Who being the brightness of his glory, and the express image of his person, and upholding all things by the word of his power, when he had by himself purged our sins, sat down on the right hand of the Majesty on high.

—Hebrews 1:3 KJV

This verse is in reference to Jesus, who is the express image of who God is. The Greek word used here for "image" is *charakter*. It means an "exact reproduction." Jesus was an exact reproduction of God. The original use for this word was to describe a tool used for engraving. It was further used to describe a mould. Today we have advanced science and technology wherein we might use the word "clone."

Scientists at the University of Edinburgh in Scotland actually cloned a sheep in 1996. They used a process known as somatic cell nuclear fusion. The clone was named Dolly. Dolly had no father. She had three mothers. One provided the egg, another the DNA, and the third carried her to birth. Dolly was an exact duplicate of the donor's DNA. After Dolly, scientists were able to clone pigs, deer, and horses. Now that we have reviewed this lesson in science, how does it apply to our faith? It's quite simple, actually: Jesus and God have the same spiritual DNA.

Jesus had a conversation with Philip, one of His disciples, in John 14:8–9: *"Philip said, 'Lord, show us the Father and that will be enough for us.' Jesus answered: 'Don't you know me, Philip, even after I have been among you such a long time? Anyone who has seen me has seen the Father. How can you say, "Show us the Father"?'"* (NIV). It is clear that Jesus is the exact image of God. If we desire to know God and His nature, we should observe how Jesus conducted Himself.

The first thing that stands out to me about Jesus is the way He displayed forgiveness. The religious leaders of that day enjoyed doling out judgment and punishment. They felt justified in doing so, and such actions may have provided them with a sense of self-righteousness. When Jesus encountered people, He boldly proclaimed that they were forgiven. The forgiveness was granted in many cases before it was even asked for. It seems like no matter what someone had done, forgiveness was automatically granted. For example, there is the story of Jesus healing someone who was paralyzed as found in Mark 2:5–12. "When Jesus saw their faith, he said to the paralyzed man, 'Son, your sins are forgiven.' Now some teachers of the law were sitting there, thinking to themselves, 'Why does this fellow talk like that? He's blaspheming! Who can forgive sins but God alone?' Immediately Jesus knew in his spirit that this was what they were thinking in their hearts, and he said to them, 'Why are you thinking these things? Which is easier: to say to this paralyzed man, "Your sins are forgiven," or to say, "Get up, take your mat and walk"? But I want you to know that the Son of

Man has authority on earth to forgive sins.' So he said to the man, 'I tell you, get up, take your mat and go home.' He got up, took his mat and walked out in full view of them all. This amazed everyone and they praised God, saying, 'We have never seen anything like this!'" (NIV). Jesus did something only God could do! *"Who forgives all your sins and heals all your diseases."* Psalm 103:3 (NIV).

The apostle Paul described it this way in 2 Corinthians 5:19: *"that God was reconciling the world to himself in Christ, not counting people's sins against them. And he has committed to us the message of reconciliation"* (NIV).

It seems counterintuitive for many mainline Christians to believe that God does not hold our sins against us. We have seen that this holds true before Jesus went to the cross, so how much more after Jesus died on the cross? Many people see God as aloof. Jesus clearly showed everyone He encountered that God is tangible and desires interaction.

The Great Physician and Healer

The next hallmark of the life of Jesus would be His ease and willingness to heal the sick.

When Jesus came down from the mountain, large crowds followed Him. And a leper came to Him and bowed down before Him, and said, "Lord, if You are willing, You can make me clean." Jesus stretched out His hand and touched him, saying, "I am willing; be cleansed." And immediately his leprosy was cleansed.

—Matthew 8:1–3 NASB

When the even was come, they brought unto him many that were possessed with devils: and he cast out the spirits with his word, and healed all that were sick: That it might be fulfilled which was spoken by Isiah the prophet, saying, Himself took our infirmities, and bare our sicknesses.

—Matthew 8:16–17 KJV

We can see that Jesus was willing and able to heal anyone from anything, thus demonstrating the nature of God in a tangible way. We can make this distinct connection because Jesus Himself said this:

"Truly, truly, I say to you, the Son can do nothing of Himself, unless it is something He sees the Father doing; for whatever the Father does, these things the Son also does in like manner."

—John 5:19 NASB

There are dozens of such illustrations in the four Gospels. It would be well worth the time to do a simple Internet search of the instances when Jesus healed the sick. Take time to notice how many times Jesus healed all who came to Him, even if the crowd was in the thousands. Jesus had one simple motivating factor for doing this: love and compassion.

Jesus went forth, and saw a great multitude, and was

moved with compassion toward them, and he healed their sick.

—Matthew 14:14 KJV

Jesus is so much more! We could easily make a list a page long. Why not make that a project of your own? Take some time and make a list of what He is to you and to others. You may use biblical references or feel free to use your own descriptive words.

5

We Are: _____

Ambassadors

We are ambassadors! Yes, we are! Everyone who has experienced the new birth and is one with Jesus is invited to become an ambassador for Him. The term is used in 1 Corinthians 5:20 and in Ephesians 6:20, where the apostle Paul said he was an ambassador in chains. The definition used in the Bible for "ambassador" means an older, mature, and venerated person. It also means to act as a statesman or a diplomat. In other words, an ambassador would represent a king and his kingdom. The mission therefore assigned to us is to become mature and very skilled at knowing our King and how He would like to be represented. We have looked at a few examples of how Jesus represented God. The natural process would be for us to represent Jesus as He represented God.

The mark of maturity can be defined in many ways, so I will just highlight a few. The ability to respond to people and situations in a calm manner is essential. The temptation to be emotionally reactive must be tempered with patience, gentleness, and kindness. The ability to listen to others and offer empathy is also a sign of maturity. Our words of response should be clear and concise. Christian clichés are not needed or helpful in most conversations. Examples of Christian clichés would include: "When God closes a door, He opens a window"; "God will not give you more than you can handle"; "Just trust in Jesus." The intention may be good, but stale, rehearsed talking points seem too shallow when someone is hurting.

Mature behavior also means we always do the right thing—always. There is much to be said about time and life experience that translate into maturity, that is, *if* we learn the lessons along the way. This helps to give us perspective. When we gain a proper perspective, it allows us to be more objective with the lens we see through. A good barometer of immaturity is to see how often someone has an emotional and subjective speaking pattern rather than a tempered and objective pattern of speech. Think about how our attitudes, speech, and behavior is perceived by others. If others feel like they have to avoid us, then we are not representing Jesus well. If others find us refreshing and light, He is pleased!

One of the best ways to represent Jesus, the Prince of Peace, is to live a life void of strife and arguments. *Webster's Dictionary* defines *strife* as "discord, *strife*, conflict, contention, dissension, a state or condition marked by a lack of agreement or harmony." Discord implies an intrinsic or essential lack of harmony producing quarreling, factiousness, or antagonism. Proverbs 20:3 says, *"It is to one's honor to avoid strife, but every fool is quick to quarrel"* (NIV). And Proverbs 10:12 says, *"Hatred stirs up conflict, but love covers over all wrongs"* (NIV). The apostle Paul addresses strife in the New Testament:

> *For ye are yet carnal: for whereas there is among you envying, and strife, and divisions, are ye not carnal, and walk as men?*
> —1 Corinthians 3:3 KJV

Here is another translation of that verse from Weymouth:

> *You are still unspiritual. For so long as jealousy and strife continue among you, can it be denied that you are unspiritual and are living and acting like mere men of the world?*

We can benefit from the context of this verse about strife as pertaining to maturity using the Passion Translation.

> *Brothers and sisters, when I was with you, I found it impossible to speak to you as those who are spiritually mature people, for you are still dominated by the mind-set of the flesh. And because you are immature infants in Christ, I had to nurse you and feed you with milk, not with the solid food of more advanced teachings, because you weren't ready for it. In fact, you are still not ready to be fed solid food, for you are living your lives dominated by the mind-set of the flesh. Ask yourselves: Is there jealousy among you? Do you compare yourselves with others? Do you quarrel like children and end up taking sides? If so, this proves that you are living*

your lives centered on yourselves, dominated by the mind-set of the flesh, and behaving like unbelievers.

—1 Corinthians 3:1–3 TPT

James 3:16 tell us, *"For where envying and strife is, there is confusion and every evil work"* (KJV). Have you ever been in a conversation where one person gets louder, then another, and soon people are interrupting each other? You can sense the tension in the room. There seems to be confusion in many cases. The whole conversation breaks down and becomes unfruitful and unprofitable. Well, that is the result of strife. James seems to indicate that this kind of conversation and behavior opens up portals to every evil work. I have seen this in the workplace, in families, at holiday events, and even at church. It is a wise person who will avoid strife. A wise person will learn how to navigate through the noise and confusion and walk in a peaceful attitude. An opportunity to practice the presence of peace (a fruit of the Spirit) is given when we encounter strife. We have a mandate to replace the earthly, lower sense of arguing with the heavenly higher realm of peace and stability. When we do this well, we are truly ambassadors of God. It is a process. It does take intentional practice and patience. It can be developed. It will change us and the world around us. This requires us to see others through a different lens. Our goal is to have a ministry of reconciliation.

The apostle Paul phrased it this way:

God was in Christ personally reconciling the world to himself—not counting their sins against them—and has commissioned us with the message of reconciliation.

—2 Corinthians 5:19 PHILLIPS

I like the Weymouth New Testament translation of this verse:

We are to tell how God was in Christ reconciling the world to Himself, not charging men's transgressions to their account, and that He has entrusted to us the Message of this reconciliation.

Paul states that this is the message we should be conveying to others. Forgiveness is the message we have been entrusted with. The too-good-to-be-true news is that the message applies to everyone, not just those who already believe. The word "reconcile" was used in accounting. Imagine if someone deposited a large sum of money into your bank account, but for some reason you never knew about it. It was there all the time, and yet you never drew upon it as a resource. To be reconciled to God is just that simple. It is already there for everyone to benefit from. Some discover the treasure, and some do not. Our mission is to help others discover this treasure that has already been deposited into their life.

6

Going to Church

What is the church? What kind of church should I attend? How often should I attend church? Should I become a member? These are just some questions that are often asked by Christians. The word *church* as used in the Bible is derived from the word *ecclesia*, which means "a congregation," "an assembly," or "called-out ones." The church is not a building nor a specific denomination. The church is comprised of people who do not merely profess faith in Jesus, but actually do their best to surrender themselves to follow Jesus who is the head of the church body.

And God placed all things under his feet and appointed him to be head over everything for the church, which is his body, the fullness of him who fills everything in every way.

—Ephesians 1:22–23 NIV

There is therefore the church universal, and then there is what is commonly known as the local church. It matters not where this body of believers meet; it is still *His* church. It does not matter how many people are gathered in a place; it is still *His* church.

There are so many different types of churches that exist, how can we decide which one to attend? I would suggest that you think outside the box and find someplace that presents an opportunity to grow in faith, grow in relationships, grow in worship, and more. Someone who is single might find they resonate with one type of church, while a family with small children might find they identify with a much different type of church. We live in a wonderful age of technology, which enables us to not merely look at the website of a church and discover their core beliefs, but also watch videos of services online through social media to get a feel for what to expect, although there is perhaps nothing better than being there in person upon a visit. I would suggest visiting many churches before making a decision as to regular attendance at one particular church. In other words, shop around! Remember, you belong to God. The institutional church is merely a place to facilitate the assembly of believers. Love, grace, peace, and forgiveness should be observable in such places, as well as structure. There simply is no such thing as a perfect church. Sound theology is important, but not nearly as important as the unity of faith. There does need to be some common essentials of the faith to be agreed upon. We can all grow in other areas of belief. We all see in part and know in part. No one person, nor one church, has it all. A church that claims to have it all and know it all should raise a red flag for you. The tragedy of the post-apostolic church is that we as a body have become so divided. The early Christian church might have had some disagreements, but there was only one church body, which met at various places. The apostle Paul would address the church at Corinth, the church at Ephesus, etc. Also, these regional churches would mostly meet at houses.

There are many models of church structures in our society, and house churches are certainly just as legitimate as any other type. While people may not agree on everything, the most important thing we can focus on is simply not to be disagreeable in our attitudes. We must learn to be body minded. We all need one another, even if we have differing points of view. There is one body, one faith, and one Lord, as stated in Ephesians 4. In that chapter, the apostle Paul gave instructions to the early Christian church:

As a prisoner of the Lord, I plead with you to walk holy, in a way that is suitable to your high rank, given to you in your divine calling. With tender humility and quiet patience, always demonstrate gentleness and generous love toward one another, especially toward those who may try your patience. Be faithful to guard the sweet harmony of the Holy Spirit among you in the bonds of peace, being one body and one spirit, as you were all called into the same glorious hope of divine destiny. For the Lord God is one, and so are we, for we share in one faith, one baptism, and one Father. And He is the perfect Father who leads us all, works through us all, and lives in us all! And he has generously given each one of us supernatural grace, according to the size of the gift of Christ. This is why he says: "He ascends into the heavenly

41

heights taking his many captured ones with him, and gifts were given to men." He "ascended" means that he returned to heaven, after he had first descended from the heights of heaven, even descending as far as the lowest parts of the earth. The same one who descended is also the one who ascended above the heights of heaven, in order to begin the restoration and fulfillment of all things. And he has appointed some with grace to be apostles, and some with grace to be prophets, and some with grace to be evangelists, and some with grace to be pastors, and some with grace to be teachers. And their calling is to nurture and prepare all the holy believers to do their own works of ministry, and as they do this they will enlarge and build up the body of Christ. These grace ministries will function until we all attain oneness in the faith, until we all experience the fullness of what it means to know the Son of God, and finally until we become one into a perfect man with the full dimensions of spiritual maturity and fully developed into the abundance of Christ. And then our immaturity will end! And we will not be easily shaken by trouble, nor led astray by novel teachings or by the false doctrines of deceivers who teach clever lies. But instead, we will remain strong and always sincere in our love as we express the truth. All our direction and ministries will flow from Christ and lead us deeper into him, the anointed Head of his body, the church. For his "body" has been formed in his image and is closely joined together and constantly connected as one. And every member has been given divine gifts to contribute to the growth of all; and as these gifts operate effectively throughout the whole body, we are built up and made perfect in love.

—Ephesians 4:1–16 TPT

How often should we attend a church? There is simply not one answer that is applicable to everyone and every situation. The tradition has been to attend at least once a week. That is something I did as a child attending a Roman Catholic church. Later as a young adult who experienced Jesus in a personal way, I attended a somewhat traditional Pentecostal church, in a denomination known as the Assemblies of God. We were encouraged to attend Sunday morning, Sunday night, and Wednesday evening services. The early Christian church would often meet daily in the local Jewish temple and enjoy meals together as they went from house to house (Acts 2:46). I think the takeaway should be a focus on real community. The age in which we live provides us with the ability and flexibility to listen to tens of thousands of sermons online anytime we desire. Many trending churches offer multiple services on the weekends. I would suggest looking at this as a process. Pray often, follow your heart, follow after peace, and have fun with it.

There are a number of religious organizations that seem more concerned with what day of the week you attend church than anything else. They tend to be dogmatic about it. This stems from a legalistic view of various passages in the Bible. A faithful believer should never feel pressured to follow such doctrines, nor feel condemned if they do not adhere to it.

What about church membership? The fledgling Christian church was largely built through relationships. Today most churches have become organized religious institutions that are defined by layers of structure, formality, policies, doctrinal stances, and hierarchy. Thousands of years of church history stand between the first and the latter. There are several lectures about church history available to anyone who is connected to the Internet. Every believer should take advantage of this information so that we have a frame of reference when navigating church life today.

The majority of churches today allow anyone to attend church services without being a member; however, if someone desires to become active in some leadership role or even a team member role, there usually are membership requirements that would have to be met. This may include attending special educational classes, interviews, and signing a member covenant agreement wherein certain expectations are spelled out and certain promises are made. A church near me that is nondenominational and evangelical has an extensive agreement form. Some of the expectations are as follows: Members are expected to give 10 percent of their gross income to the church (known as a tithe), even when on vacation; members are expected to attend all weekly and special services and not attend another church if the times conflict; members are expected to volunteer their time and services on a regular basis; and members are expected to live up to moral standards as set forth by the church, which are based on the Bible.

This may seem extreme to some, but for others it is a matter of course. Not all churches set forth such demands, but this does seem to be a trend in churches that are trendy. There are some churches that simply ask that you sign a paper stating that you agree with the doctrinal stances held by the church and that you commit to be a part of that church family. Obviously, the early Christian church held to no such practices, yet there are some practical aspects of being an official member in a modern society. People tend to live very busy lifestyles. We live in a twenty-four-hour, seven-days-a-week world. We live in a global economy and a technological age. Structure and organization in a church can be a tremendous tool if used properly. It is important in any family that everyone be on the same page and have effective communication. The problem that often occurs is defining the line where autonomy and personal responsibility are maintained, thereby avoiding control and conformity.

So we, being many, are one body in Christ, and every one members one of another.
—Romans 12:5 KJV

There is a tremendous need for church leaders to recognize this spiritual reality, that we have been qualified as members simply by the evidence of our genuine faith in Jesus. The apostle Paul relates this concept in chapter 12 of 1 Corinthians. Please take the time to read the entire chapter from this New Testament book in order to gain a more organic perspective in defining membership. You can buy a print version of the Bible or find a version online; you can even download a Bible version app to your phone or other device. Ideally, we should be able to visit any church anywhere in the world and be openly accepted as a member of *His* Church.

Online church services became the norm as a result of the 2020 pandemic. This required quite an adjustment for all of us. The church was able to survive, and some churches even thrived despite this huge and challenging transition. The sense of community was perhaps the factor most missed during this time. Going to church in many ways had to be redefined, and so we should not place the church in a box lest we miss what the church is to begin with.

7

The Tree of Life

Most people are familiar with the story of the garden of Eden.

And the LORD God planted a garden eastward in Eden; and there he put the man whom he had formed. And out of the ground made the LORD God to grow every tree that is pleasant to the sight, and good for food; the tree of life also in the midst of the garden, and the tree of knowledge of good and evil.

—Genesis 2:8–9 KJV

The Hebrew word used to define "life" is *chayah*. It means "to nourish, to keep alive, to make alive." This deserves understanding as we fast-forward to when Jesus walked the earth. The Tree of Life is actually a type and shadow of Jesus who was planted into the garden of humanity at the appointed time. In fact, Jesus spoke these words:

For had ye believed Moses, ye would have believed me; for he wrote of me.

—John 5:46 KJV

Man shall not live by bread alone, but by every word that proceeds out of the mouth of God.

—Matthew 4:4 NKJV

It is the Spirit who gives life; the flesh profits nothing; the words that I have spoken to you are spirit and are life.

—John 6:63 NASB

I am the way and the truth and the life. No one comes to the Father except through me.

—John 14:6 NIV

Jesus was clearly telling those who knew the Jewish faith that *He is the Tree of Life*, and furthermore His words are the Tree of Life as well. There are two principles that define organic Christian life. When we learn them and practice them well, many other facets of life tend to fall into place.

Principle 1: Living from the inside out

Most people conform to a set of rules that are imposed on them believing that how well someone does this makes them closer to God or a good Christian. Allowing Jesus to live His life in us and through us is a completely different dynamic. The apostle Paul stated it this way:

I have been crucified with Christ. It is no longer I who live, but Christ who lives in me. And the life I now live in the flesh I live by faith in the Son of God, who loved me and gave himself for me.

—Galatians 2:20 ESV

It is possible to be so connected to Jesus that His life nourishes us, sustains us, inspires us, helps us, and guides us. He is a Tree of Life for us. We become "Jesus with skin on," so to speak, and others can tell. The Passion Translation of Galatians 2:20 really spells this out:

My old identity has been co-crucified with Messiah and no longer lives; for the nails of his cross crucified me with him. And now the essence of this new life is no longer mine, for the Anointed One lives his life through me—we live in union as one! My new life is empowered by the faith of the Son of God who loves me so much that he gave himself for me, and dispenses his life into mine!

We do not need to employ religious gymnastics to accomplish this goal. Have you ever stood by an apple orchard and listened to the trees? Why? you might ask. Well, it may seem silly, but you will not hear much at all. The trees produce the delicious fruit seemingly without effort. The spiritual fruit we produce is accomplished in like manner. The kind of fruit grown through us by being connected to Jesus is love, joy, peace, patience, kindness, gentleness, goodness, and self-control (Galatians 5:22). This is far more than natural emotions being expressed. I recall the first day I was saved, the spiritual fruit of love permeated my entire being. That is partaking of the fruit from the Tree of Life—tapping into the sap within, so to speak.

I also remember times when I felt the evidence of peace inside me that was so deep, it was like I was swimming in it. There have been days when I feel like I am in another atmosphere than everyone else around me. The atmosphere of peace is created when it has been digested from the Tree of Life.

There is a unique correlation between natural bodily digestion and spiritual digestion. Both require a proper balance of nutrients. God supplies the natural and spiritual food in many ways. It is our responsibility to make the effort to ensure we eat well. With regard to reading and partaking of the table of the Word of God, the Bible, one way I found that is highly practical is to ask myself, how does this apply to my life in a way that brings life to me? If the Word of God does not bring life and peace to the reader, then it is being misunderstood, applied incorrectly, or erroneously interpreted. I discovered a very useful tool in this regard. I purchased a book that explained the customs and cultures of the land and times to which the Bible relates. This was a tremendous help to me and caused my understanding to be relevant to life. It also helped me to avoid the trap of being legalistic as to the Bible and my faith. Thinking about context, customs, and culture can keep you on the road and out of the ditch. I have seen that most of the Christian community relate to God by following the Bible, as well as applying sermons they have heard. There is, however, perhaps nothing greater than talking to Jesus like you would talk to a friend. The art of conversation is not just talking but listening with the heart as well as the ears. This is often called fellowship. People who spend a lot of time together begin to know each other well. Deep and intimate conversation creates deep, meaningful, and lasting bonds. Relationships like this bring about influence and change. In other words, the traits of the other person rub off on us. Relating to Jesus this way is where spiritual impartation occurs. As if He were a pitcher and we were a drinking glass, He begins to pour His virtue into us. Our capacity to be filled will help us to become more like Him. We feel His feelings and think His thoughts. We are aware of His presence, and it changes how we live and move and have our being. Hopefully we are so filled by Him that it begins to overflow onto others. Our existence is sustained by the Tree of Life, and thus we grow day by day so that we become the same for others.

Principle 2. Being a tree of life to others

Have you ever experienced a conversation wherein a person seems to talk at you instead of with you? A person who is a religious zealot often has this tendency. I say "religious" because this applies to any religion. I specifically did not refer to someone who has a passionate faith in Jesus, because if we are completely surrendered to Him, we will act like He did and conduct ourselves in such a fashion as to draw people into the love of God rather than repel them with religious thought. One way to leave a bitter taste behind us is to speak in our own religious language, dubbed "Christianese." Jesus did not speak King James English in His conversations, and neither should we.

Jesus did not come to condemn the world, and neither should we (John 3:17). Everyone we meet has some issue they are dealing with. Some of the most painful wounds are the wounds that are not seen. We need to meet people where they are and bring them the hope of finding purpose and meaning in life. When a Christian throws out formulaic and stale solutions, it most likely will not help. Worse yet is when a Christian comes across as arrogant and superior and belittles others. Humility is a wonderful virtue to embrace when talking to others. Love, mercy, forgiveness, gentleness, kindness, and grace should be our calling card. This is also true when interacting with other believers. When two or more believers are talking and disagreements occur, the conversation often deteriorates into what I call a "Bible battle." This need not be a way of life for any believer. We can and will sometimes disagree, yet we do not need to be disagreeable in our attitudes and mannerisms. The written Word of God is referred to as a sword (Hebrews 4:12). We can use it to cut or to heal. The key to using this sword to reach the human soul is this:

Who also hath made us able ministers of the new testament; not of the letter, but of the spirit: for the letter killeth, but the spirit giveth life.
—2 Corinthians 3:6 KJV

Another way of looking at this is to do all we can to ensure that when we speak to anyone, we bring them words of life and perhaps even a refreshing word in due season. The same words from the Bible can be used to bind someone or to set them free. The difference is how we frame the words and also the spirit behind the words we use. Tension in our conversation may be an indicator as to the heart attitudes that lurk behind our words. We see an example of this with the disciples of Jesus:

When His disciples James and John saw this, they said, "Lord, do You want us to command fire to come down from heaven and consume them?" But He turned and rebuked them, and said, "You do not know what kind of spirit you are of."

—Luke 9:54–55 NASB

We should be aware of what virtues are working in us and through us as our day unfolds and we encounter people and situations.

One of the most fascinating ways to be a transformative influence is to practice the presence of God. That is to allow ourselves to become aware of the hidden treasure within us, the Holy Spirit.

And if the Spirit of Him who raised up Jesus from the dead is dwelling in you, He who raised up Christ from the dead will give Life also to your mortal bodies because of His Spirit who dwells in you.

—Romans 8:11 WEYMOUTH

Our awareness of His presence dwelling in us allows Him to emanate from us like a magnetic field so that others may benefit from the Tree of Life.

For we are God's fellow workers [His servants working together]; you are God's cultivated field [His garden, His vineyard], God's building.

—1 Corinthians 3:9 AMP

Anyone who has planted and maintained a garden knows how much time and attention it takes to produce the desired results. Take the time and make the effort to work on your own garden, which is really His garden. Do your absolute best to keep it free from weeds and pests. The tree of life stood among all the other trees as mentioned in Genesis. These trees were pleasant to behold and good for food. Likewise, as we become a tree of life for others, they should find us pleasant and nourishing to the soul.

8

Growing in the Grace Walk

"Amazing grace, how sweet the sound, that saved a wretch like me." Most people have heard the opening words of this old song. The grace of God is amazing. It is almost too good to be true. It is undeniable when encountered. Ephesians 2:8 states, *"For it is by grace you have been saved, through faith—and this is not from yourselves, it is the gift of God"* (NIV). Grace is simply defined as "favor that is not earned," and "kindness." This is the normative method of operation (MO) for God. He extends His unmerited favor and kindness to us with the expectation that we will respond with full acceptance in genuine faith.

Historically, the majority of those in the Christian faith tend to measure how well they are doing based on performance. In other words, how well someone keeps the rules, what they should do and what they should not do, to them, determines how much God approves of them or would bless them. The blessings of God, according to this view, depends totally on human obedience and performance. Many times, if someone encountered a difficult life circumstance, others would presume and accuse that person of having done something that did not please God. The grace of God seemed to be a missing equation in the life of a believer aside from being saved. The most transformative biblical principle for me and my wife was discovered the year we transitioned from a performance-based faith to a grace-based faith. We began to look at the topic and search the Bible for the practical application of how God extends His grace to us.

For the law was given by Moses, but grace and truth came by Jesus Christ.

—John 1:7 KJV

The Word became flesh and made his dwelling among us. We have seen his glory, the glory of the one and only Son, who came from the Father, full of grace and truth.

—John 1:14 NIV

For He it is from whose fullness we have all received, and grace upon grace.

—John 1:16 WEYMOUTH

Moreover the law entered, that the offense might abound. But where sin abounded, grace did much more abound.

—Romans 5:20 KJV

We began to see that the favor of God is not predicated upon our perfection or lack thereof. We no longer viewed

God as a giant whack-a-mole player who was just waiting for someone to mess up so He could bop them on the head. In fact, it is a throne of grace we are encouraged to boldly approach when we need help, not one of judgment. Hebrews 4:16 (KJV) instructs:

Let us therefore come boldly unto the throne of grace, that we may obtain mercy, and find grace to help in time of need.

We began to see others who had issues through a different lens. The message we now are entrusted with is that when sin abounds in a life, the grace of God for that person is greater than the sin. We tend to categorize sinful behavior. The wonder of the cross is this: The greater the sin, the greater the grace that is extended. In other words, there is nothing that Jesus cannot forgive and cleanse. We may have consequences here on earth, but in heaven we have a court system that is based on mercy, grace, forgiveness, redemption, and restoration. Some biblical scholars have framed this heavenly court in these simple terms: God is the judge of all, yet He is a merciful judge. Jesus is our lawyer, or advocate. The evidence on earth may find us guilty, but the court finds us blameless. We are set free!

My little children, I am writing these things to you so that you may not sin. And if anyone sins, we have an Advocate with the Father, Jesus Christ the righteous.

—1 John 2:1 NASB

The one verse about grace that captured me the most is 2

Peter 3:18: *"But grow in grace, and in the knowledge of our Lord and Saviour Jesus Christ"* (KJV). The word *grow* may also be translated as "increase." To increase in grace requires us to be intentional in our daily applications.

The cry of our heart should be one of asking God to reveal how we can grow in grace within our circle of influence. I have found this to be a learning process. It is okay to make mistakes along the way. The key is to learn from those mistakes and not repeat them. Take time to review the days and weeks and ask yourself how you could have shown more grace to yourself and others. Take this on as a quest. Make it a mission statement: "I will grow in grace. I will increase my ability to understand it and use it every day."

To grow in the knowledge of Jesus in this context is to gain firsthand personal experience as opposed to secondhand information. This has often been compared to reading so much about a famous person that one feels they know a lot about them, but that is secondhand knowledge. Firsthand knowledge is to actually spend time with the person and know them as a best friend or lover. Our goal therefore should be to grow in knowing God and to grow in grace. We can easily assess our progress by asking the question, "Do I have more grace today in my life, or less grace?"

9

What About the Money Thing?

Most people catch on pretty quick that it seems like churches spend too much time asking for money. It often gives the impression that the underlying motivation for bringing people to church is to fill up more seats and obtain more money so they can build bigger buildings that can hold more people who can give more money so they can build yet another building.

The human ego may play a part in the pursuit of having the biggest church in town, but only God knows the true condition of the heart. We should therefore be careful not to judge. We do have a responsibility to give our money, time, and energy into something we believe is genuine, an organization that is spending money wisely. We may choose to give to a large church because of the impact they can make on a region. We may choose to give to a small church because we find real community and love there. We may choose to give to an Internet-based ministry because we find inspiration and are challenged to grow through the instruction we receive. We may choose to give to a charity that is making a real difference and helping others. The most important matter is not where we give, but that we have a genuine attitude of gratitude for whatever we do have and we are willing to share some of our resources with others. This is often referred to as a spirit of generosity. Anyone can do this, because anyone can be a giver, no matter how much or how little they have.

I was making a delivery to an auto parts store one day. There was a line at the register, and the phone was ringing. The store was short on staff. There was a customer who began to cause a problem. He was yelling at the workers. He wanted them to take care of him first even though he was at the back of the line. His major complaint was that He required a taxi to get to the store in order to buy the part to fix his car and the taxi was waiting for him. He was in a panic because he only had so much money to pay the taxi driver. The time spent in the store could make him owe more than what he had on him. I started to talk to this person, and I offered to pay for the taxi if he would be willing to wait patiently in line with the others. He was taken back for a moment but agreed to do so, thereby resolving a very tense situation. Arguments turned into peace, all because of a little generosity.

Concerning giving among the Christian community, the apostle Paul gave some very practical instruction in 2 Corinthians 8–9. You may want to take the time to read those chapters carefully. Please note that in the context, Paul is talking about a collection for the poor in another region. The collection is not for a building, nor for the salaries of church leaders. This obvious fact is sometimes overlooked. I would highlight 2 Corinthians 8:12 as well as 9:7. Consider various translations to get a clear picture, and what you will discover is an instruction to *give as one chooses* in the heart and to give *in proportion to what one can afford*. Compare this to what most churches teach about giving, and you will find a stark difference.

For those who are involved in a church and feel compelled to give to that church, I have a few suggestions. Let us state the obvious: Bills need to be paid and paid on time. A church that provides a safe and comfortable place to gather is worthy of financial support, especially if the facility is well maintained and used often and for many different purposes.

There is a temptation for church leaders who oversee what are known as megachurches to engage in the abuse of money. Many pastors who hold such positions live the lifestyle of the wealthy while others in the church struggle to provide for a family. I would find it difficult to give my hard-earned money to such an organization. Money is sometimes raised through guilt and manipulation. Do not fall for such tactics.

Most pastors are there because they love God and love people. Most pastors are not greedy. Most pastors have a genuine desire to help the community in which they live. Most pastors will teach what is commonly known as the tithe. That is where every member of the church is expected to give 10 percent of their income to the church as an obligation. I recently heard one pastor tell a church that generosity begins at 11 percent. I have heard others state that if a Christian does not tithe, they will be cursed. There is a lot of really bad teaching on the subject, and anyone would be wise to read up on it objectively. I have found that there is a tendency to read *into* the Bible what we have already been taught through a preconceived opinion. This causes us to make the Bible say something that it actually does *not* say. We therefore blindly follow the traditional teaching as they have been passed down. Pastors are usually incorrectly taught concerning the tithe when they attend a Bible college and rarely see it from a different perspective.

Honestly, it is easy to understand how a pastor needs the congregation to tithe because all too often their own income depends on it. So, does God require us to tithe? The answer is no. Did Jesus teach His disciples to tithe? The answer is no. Did any of the apostles teach the early church to tithe? The answer is no. Then why is it so commonly taught? There may be several reasons, but the most obvious to me is a misunderstanding of the initial purpose of a mandatory tithe. The Jewish people were a nation unto themselves. It was a theocratic nation. The tithe was, for the most part, used as a way to support the centralized temple and the priesthood. Some of the tithe was used to support the poor and needy, much like a welfare system. We no longer have a centralized temple, nor do we have a priesthood as it were, who act as mediators between us and God. There are a few religious denominations who still have priests who act as mediators, but most models of the Christian faith believe that Jesus instituted a new covenant wherein He Himself is the mediator. Along side this many countries have a welfare system provided by the government which is paid for by taxes.

This covenant between God and humans is based upon the sacrifice Jesus made. There is no longer a need for a centralized temple, nor is there a need for a religious order of priests. In short, *Jesus changed everything.* Yet many churches today fail to see that this change includes the tithe. Most pastors will quote Malachi 3 as a persuasive passage from the Bible. It would behoove Christians to read the entire chapter and ask some pointed questions, such as: Does this really apply to Christians today? How did Jesus dying on the cross affect how we are blessed or cursed today? If the tithe was to be brought into the storehouse, is it fair to imply that a local church is the storehouse? Jesus did tell the Pharisees, who were under the law of Moses and who used the temple, that they should not neglect the tithe, but where is it recorded that Jesus taught His own disciples to tithe? Jesus taught crowds who numbered in the thousands, but did He tell these common people to tithe?

Lastly, believers should do a word search in the New Testament books, starting with the book of Acts, because that is where we discover the early church and the apostles' teachings. How many times does the subject of the tithe occur in these books? The answer is: very few. Furthermore, when the tithe is mentioned, it is always in reference to the Jewish nation and Abraham. Some have contended that we should tithe because Abraham tithed to someone called Melchizedek, and this was before the time of the temple and the priesthood. It seems that this story also has been misread and misapplied. The first item that should stand out like a sore thumb is that Abraham did not use his own money with which to tithe. He tithed from the spoils of a war that he had won. Furthermore, it appears that God never instructed him to do so, and thus this tithe was completely voluntary. It should be also noted that while most churches believe the subject of the story is the tithe, the *true* subject of the story is the character named Melchizedek. This character is a type and shadow of Jesus Himself.

Types and shadows are widely used throughout the Bible, especially in the Old Testament books. They all point to Jesus, the Lamb of God who takes away the sins of the world (John 1:29). The study of types and shadows is a fascinating way to discover and unlock the deeper meanings of Scripture. For example, in the Ten Commandments, we find an instruction to keep the sabbath day of rest, as a day to enter into rest. Jesus walked the earth and proclaimed that we should come to Him and He would give us rest. Rest is no longer a day, but a Person. In other words, the day of rest was a shadow, but Jesus is the substance. Likewise, the tithe was but a mere shadow of the One who gave His life as a first fruit offering. Thus, we conclude that Jesus became our sin, our rest, and our tithe. He is our high priest, and we are now the temple of God. (Hebrews 4–10 would be well worth reading for biblical perspective concerning this.)

All this being said, it is also acceptable for someone to tithe if that is what they have in their heart to do. To give from the heart is a wonderful expression of gratitude. To give to something you believe in is a noble gesture. I would offer some advice for those who wish to tithe. We are not under an obligation to tithe. God will not be angry at us if we give less than 10 percent, but if you desire to tithe, please make sure you have financial stability before doing so. Why? Because it presents a rather poor witness to others if we tithe, yet cannot pay our own bills. Actually, not to pay the bills on time is being irresponsible. God would be more pleased if we keep our word and our commitments. If we have debt of any kind, that is something we promised to pay back. We should do everything we can to do so in a timely manner. We may have to move to a smaller place and spend less money in order to live within our income. Sometimes tragic and unplanned situations happen, and God understands these things as well.

There are some who teach that you can tithe your way out of debt. This teaching is based on the principle of sowing and reaping. Jesus did teach about sowing a lot, and so did the apostles after Jesus died and the church began to increase.

We should always be looking for opportunities to sow a seed of blessing to someone in need. In fact, there are some who practice a lifestyle of minimalism so that they can maximize their resources, either in savings and retirement or in generosity. One must decide for themselves what is best, as each one of us is accountable to God to seek for direction and guidance. We all experience seasons in life. The more we can gain a broader perspective, the better. Only God knows the beginning from the end, but it helps to understand that not everything is a crisis. We must learn to trust the process of learning in all things, even with money.

The Christian life is not a math formula; therefore, exercise caution when presented with such teachings. Just because we do steps 1, 2, and 3, that does not guarantee that results X, Y, and Z will happen. Do good with all that you have. Be willing to learn. Trust that God will lead you by His Spirit. Let no one judge you.

10

Pardon Me

The one subject most people struggle with is *forgiveness.* Here is a list of synonyms for forgiveness: *pardon, absolution, exoneration, remission, mercy.* Psychologists generally define *forgiveness* as a conscious, deliberate decision to release feelings of resentment or vengeance toward a person or group who has harmed you, regardless of whether they actually deserve your forgiveness. To grant forgiveness therefore requires being decisive. A practical example would be someone who files for bankruptcy. The court makes a decision and grants forgiveness of the debt owed. The slate is wiped clean.

The first step in giving and receiving forgiveness is to become absolutely decisive about it. This may include forgiving yourself for mistakes made. Some may need to forgive life circumstances for what feels unfair. Some may need to forgive religion for failing them. Some may need to forgive parents and other relatives for various reasons. Many find a sense of release when they name each one and grant each one forgiveness for specific offenses. It is often recommended to have a quiet space to do this in and speak the words so that they register in your mind. The main thing is to be decisive about it. The feelings will follow as time passes. I have adopted a dual approach to the subject, the human and the divine. Let us consider the latter first.

In whom we have redemption through his blood, the forgiveness of sins, according to the riches of his grace.

—Ephesians 1:7 KJV

These words, penned by the apostle Paul, are rich with meaning. "In whom" refers to Jesus. *Redemption* is defined as a release effected by the payment of a ransom. The payment took place when Jesus gave up His body and shed His innocent blood as a sacrifice for humanity. Forgiveness, according to the Greek lexicon, is defined as a release, dismissal, or pardon of a false step. The phrase "riches of His grace" may also be stated as "the wealth of His grace." The full impact of divine forgiveness is realized when it is simply accepted as a fact. No matter what the offense has been, divine forgiveness has already been granted by a previous payment made. The release occurs when the offender openly accepts the forgiveness by the action of heartfelt remorse. Divine forgiveness cannot be earned; it is simply granted to whomever has the ability to receive the gracious act.

The act of forgiveness is to release someone from the punishment deserved. I have found it necessary at times to act out the process as if the person was in front of me. I would say something like, "I release you from judgment and anger. You are free to go. I pray you may grow into a better person because kindness will lead you into a better path." I may ask God to release them, not because they deserve it, but because it is a gift that I am bestowing upon them and consequently upon myself. Not to forgive creates a self-imposed prison. It places us in a negative force that may control us, if not counteracted. The offending party may go about their life oblivious or even nonchalant as to what they have done, while we are bound in a never-ending pattern of negative thoughts and feelings. So, who is being punished, really, when we do not grant the selfless gift of absolute forgiveness? The art of living a life where forgiving is a constant stream that flows through us, releases both us and those around us. We are literally released from darkness and move into light. We are transformed from negative energy into positive energy. We become more pleasant to be around. We become more like the master of forgiveness, Jesus.

Forgiveness and healing often go hand in hand. Psalm 103:3 describes the Lord as the One *"who forgives all your sins and heals all your diseases"* (KJV). Jesus demonstrated this in His earthly ministry many times. First, He would tell someone they were forgiven. This was a new concept for the people of that time. A plethora of religious rituals were needed in order to obtain some level of pardon. Many who were not Jewish would themselves implore many gods at the other temples of idol worship. Jesus released people from guilt with a word. Many were shocked at this new practice and sharply criticized Him. Jesus was not moved and in fact went way beyond what most thought was possible. He doubled down and with a word also healed the ones He just forgave. This in itself can be considered a fulfillment of the words recorded hundreds of years prior in this psalm.

Scientific research has also correlated forgiveness and health. Harboring anger and hostility were associated with a higher risk of coronary heart disease in a paper that was published in the *Journal of the American College of Cardiology* in 2009. Studies have found that the act of forgiveness can reap huge rewards for your health: lowering the risk of heart attack; improving cholesterol levels and sleep; and reducing pain, blood pressure, and levels of anxiety, depression, and stress. And research points to an increase in the forgiveness-health connection as you age.

"There is an enormous physical burden to being hurt and disappointed," says Karen Swartz, M.D, director of the Mood Disorders Adult Consultation Clinic at The Johns Hopkins Hospital. Chronic anger puts you into a fight-or-flight mode, which results in numerous changes in heart rate, blood pressure, and immune response. Those changes, then, increase the risk of depression, heart disease, and diabetes, among other conditions. Forgiveness, however, calms stress levels, leading to improved health.

Forgiveness, whether human or divine, is a powerful force designed to help us navigate life. I suggest we take full advantage and learn them both well. There is a beautiful story in the Bible that demonstrates this in a remarkable and consequential way. It is the story of the stoning of a disciple named Stephen. The details are found in the New Testament book of Acts, chapter 7.

Stephen was a deacon in the early church who spoke boldly about Jesus, and many miracles were done by Stephen. The religious leaders, led by Saul of Tarsus, found Stephen and dragged him outside the city:

When they heard these things, they were cut to the heart, and they gnashed on him with their teeth. But he, being full of the Holy Ghost, looked up steadfastly into heaven, and saw the glory of God, and Jesus standing on the right hand of God, and said, Behold, I see the heavens opened, and the Son of man standing on the right hand of God. Then they cried out with a loud voice, and stopped their ears, and ran upon him with one accord, and cast him out of the city, and stoned him: and the witnesses laid down their clothes at a young man's feet, whose name was Saul, and they stoned Stephen, calling upon God, and saying, Lord Jesus, receive my spirit. And he kneeled down, and cried with a loud voice, Lord, lay not this sin to their charge.

—Acts 7:54–60 KJV

In other words, he forgave them. Imagine you or I being in that position. It is believed Stephen was just thirty-nine years old when this occurred.

Would we say such words in that moment? The rest of this story of forgiveness can be found in the conversion of Saul.

You can read about it in Acts 9. Saul experienced a visitation from Jesus. He experienced grace and forgiveness in spite of approving the killing of Stephen and others. He is best known as the apostle Paul, and he also performed miracles and founded many regional churches. The amazing power of forgiveness truly has actual momentum to change the future.

I would be remiss if I failed to mention the need for establishing healthy boundaries, especially when you are connected to toxic relationships. We should be careful as to the situations in which we place ourselves. We do not have to allow someone who is abusive to be close to us.

There are so many resources available to learn how to structure healthy relationships and healthy boundaries that it is not necessary to do so here. Please take the time to read up on the subject even if you do not feel you need to. You may learn some useful concepts for someone else in need.

11

How to View the Bible

"The Bible says…" Christians use this phrase often as a way to communicate what they believe God has to say concerning any number of subjects. The Bible as we know it is comprised of sixty-six books, which are divided into two sections: the Old Testament and the New Testament. Both testaments have undergone changes over the centuries, including the publication of the King James Bible in 1611. There are some who contend this version is the best and most reliable among translations in English. Most of the Christian churches do not hold the same view. One item to consider is this: What version did people read before 1611? Also, what Bible did the early Christian church have? A brief history lesson will help here.

It was during the reign of Hezekiah of Judah, in the eighth century BC that historians believe what would become the Old Testament began to take form, the result of royal scribes recording royal history and heroic legends. During the reign of Josiah, in the sixth century BC, the books of Deuteronomy and Judges were compiled and added. The final form of the Hebrew Bible developed over the next two hundred years, when Judah was swallowed up by the expanding Persian Empire. Following Persia's conquest by Alexander the Great, the Hebrew Bible was translated into *Greek* in the third century BC. This version, known as the *Septuagint*, was the version of the Old Testament used by the early Christians in Rome.

The rule of thumb, therefore, is to use a Hebrew concordance when reading the Old Testament, because this was the original language used, and to use a Greek concordance when reading the twenty-seven books that comprise the New Testament. The letters written by the apostle Paul began to circulate between 50 and 60 AD. The four Gospels began to be circulated about 70 AD, nearly forty years after Jesus died.

The book of John and the book of Revelation, also attributed to John, was written between 90 and 100 AD. However, there is some speculation that Revelation may have been written just before the fall of Jerusalem in 70 AD—a fall that Jesus predicted.

The earliest known attempt to create a canon in the same respect as the New Testament was made in the second century in Rome by Marcion, a Turkish businessman and church leader.

The Muratorian Canon, which is believed to date to 200 AD, is the earliest compilation of canonical texts resembling the New Testament. The Council of Nicea was held in 325

AD, during which the Bible as we know it came into form. It still took another two hundred years before most Christian churches came to a basic agreement on the biblical canon.

In 382 AD, a pope named Damasus commissioned a definitive Latin version of the Bible called the Vulgate. This eventually became the version used by the entire Western church. The intention in translating the Hebrew and Greek into Latin was to make the Bible more available to ordinary Christians. This, however, did not play out well, as most of Christian Europe began speaking German, French, and Spanish. The end result was that the highly educated ultimately became the elites who could read the Bible; this, of course, would include the priests.

Martin Luther worked on translating the Bible into German around 1520. William Tyndale translated the Bible into English from 1524 to 1526. He printed three thousand copies and shipped them to England, where most of the copies were seized and burned by the Bishop of London. Tyndale continued his work until he was eventually accused of being a heretic, sentenced to death, and then burned at the stake in 1536. The King James English Bible was worked on by forty-seven scholars between 1604 and 1611, with Tyndale's work being a major influence. Today we not only have printed versions of the Bible, but versions are available online and as apps that can be downloaded to our phones. What a price was paid for those who read and enjoy the Bible today!

There are now over fifty versions of the English Bible

available. Why so many? Why not just one? The answer is somewhat complex, but to frame it in simple terms, the English language cannot adequately convey the rich meanings and nuances of the original languages. Diversity of population and cultures is another reason for the adaptations, created to encourage all people to read the Bible. Some versions focus on the accuracy of a word-for-word translation. Other versions are more concerned with a thought-for-thought concept of translation. Still others express a concern to be relevant to modern vernacular. The message is the main point. The method differs. We must also realize that what was recorded thousands of years ago was written with a continual thought. None of the books had the chapter and verse breakdowns that we see today. Modern translators created that for our ease of reference.

So, why do we refer to the Bible as the Word of God? How should we interpret it?

Above all, you must understand that no prophecy of Scripture came about by the prophet's own interpretation of things. For prophecy never had its origin in the human will, but prophets, though human, spoke from God as they were carried along by the Holy Spirit.

—2 Peter 1:20–21 NIV

And we also thank God continually because, when you received the word of God, which you heard from us, you accepted it not as a human word, but as it actually is, the word of God, which is indeed at work in you who believe.

—1 Thessalonians 2:13 NIV

The Bible is more than just a record of history. Yet the telling of the stories of real people who made mistakes, as well as did great things, in itself can teach us principles to live by. The Bible becomes easier to understand when we view it through the lens of how God works with humanity with all of our inherent faults and weaknesses. Yes, imperfect people wrote the words of Scripture, first by oral tradition and tablets, then by ink and scroll, but they were being inspired by the Holy Spirit to do so. Some were fully aware of the source, and some were completely unaware of the unseen force behind what they penned. The picture often used in this thought is that of someone being in a river. The current moves them along from one place to another. They are being carried by something larger than themselves. The river of spiritual influence results in inspired thoughts couched in books and letters held together by a common thread.

Picture in your mind going back in time and trying to have a conversation with biblical characters about cars, planes, computers, cell phones, etc. Would they have any frame of reference for what you were conveying? Would they "get it"? Would they be confused? Well, we tend to do something in similar fashion when we interpret the Bible according to our current existence in a modern world culture. We tend to read into the Bible and extract conclusions without relating to the cultures of the past with all its traditions and ways of life.

I was fortunate enough to find a book about the customs and cultures of Bible lands when I was young in the faith. That one book helped me to gain perspective I would not have had simply by reading a story in the English Bible. It is amazing how this one tool can change our narrow interpretation into something meaningful that deepens our faith.

Covenants between people is something we no longer think of in terms of their usage. Yet that is exactly what the theme of the entire Bible is. The story of Noah and the ark is a fine example of a covenant. God spoke to Noah about the rainbow and called it the symbol of a covenant. In other words, God made a promise to humanity.

The wedding ceremony is another great example of a covenant promise. Each person reads or states the wedding vow, or promise. In fact, in many vows the phrase, "I promise" is often spoken. Two people enter into a covenant with each other. The key to understanding how the entire Bible relates to us is this *marriage perspective.* Concealed within the history and stories of the Old Testament (covenant) are the spiritual promises of the New Testament (covenant). It is quite interesting to note that the apostle Paul, in writing to the Corinthian church, promised or espoused them to one husband, namely Jesus, the anointed one (2 Corinthians 11:2).

It has been said by many that Jesus can be found on almost every page of the Bible. On the surface, this may seem to be exaggerated, but think about some famous stories, such as the description of the Garden of Eden. The Tree of Life was set in the midst of the garden. Jesus stated that He is the way, the truth, and the life (John 14:6).

Jesus also said that the words He spoke are life (John 6:63). The apostle Paul once referred to Christians as the garden of God (1 Corinthian 3:9). The hidden meaning of the Tree of Life can be clearly seen in the person of Jesus, as I mentioned in chapter 7 of this book. He is the Tree of Life who is in the midst of His church, the body of Christ. Thus, we have the Old Testament concealed and the New Testament revealed. Other types and shadows that point to Jesus can be seen in the stories of Moses and Abraham and David, as well as many others. This one key alone will help unravel some misunderstandings when you are reading the Bible. My advice is to look for Jesus and see how God works with people to establish His covenant with them throughout history.

The use of parables, poetry, allegory, and idiomatic sayings, as well as the use of past, present, and future prophetic writings all factor in when utilizing proper biblical exegesis. This will help determine what we take literally, what should be an objective lesson, whom we should apply it to, when it is applicable, and how we interpret what is being said. Remember, we are reading something that was written thousands of years ago, yet something that is ageless.

Psalm 22 contains most of the above-mentioned components. It is a song written by King David. The words are both poetic and speaking of future events, though at the time, this was not known. Many verses were fulfilled word for word when Jesus was crucified. This psalm is believed to have been written around 587 BC. That means six hundred years later, the prophetic words came to pass.

Isaiah 53 is another great example of prophecy as it relates to the inspiration of the Bible. This book was written about 740 BC. The entire chapter would be fulfilled over seven hundred years later in Jesus as He was crucified. You may want to pause here and read this entire chapter to comprehend the full impact of this idea. You can download the Bible app, search for Isaiah 53 online, or use a printed Bible if you have one.

There are numerous examples of such inspiration all throughout the Bible. Jesus Himself gave prophecies that came to pass. The most well-known one of these is when Jesus predicted the destruction of the Jewish temple: *"Look, Teacher, what wonderful stones and what wonderful buildings!" And Jesus said to him, "Do you see these great buildings? There will not be left here one stone upon another that will not be thrown down"* (Mark 13:1–2 KJV).

In 70 AD, some thirty-seven years after Jesus made this prediction, Rome sacked Jerusalem and destroyed it. The historian Josephus actually witnessed the siege and aftermath, and wrote these words:

Now as soon as the army had no more people to slay or to plunder, because there remained none to be the objects of their fury, Titus Caesar gave orders that they should now demolish the entire city and Temple.

Between 70 and 135 AD, the Roman soldiers stripped the Temple Mount bare, and every stone was thrown down, precisely as Jesus predicted. These examples ought to give us confidence that the Bible is a book that is truly God breathed and filled with inspiration. We should read it with an open heart and mind, willing to learn.

One last item bears repeating. The Bible was written in languages that are rich in nuances. Our English translations often miss the mark in capturing these subtle, yet meaningful differences. Reading the Bible with an open mind includes taking the time to research the original word usage. There are a number of tools available to accomplish this that are easily accessible to anyone, including the *Strong's Exhaustive Concordance for Hebrew and Greek*, a Greek lexicon, and the use of Bible apps online or downloaded for a comparison and contrast of many versions.

12

Spiritual Gifts

Most of us enjoy receiving a gift. There is such diversity in the world as to talents and abilities. These gifts to humanity often need nurturing and determined practice to become highly developed. Some may consider these abilities to be natural, yet many feel these talents are God-given from birth. *"Every good thing given and every perfect gift is from above, coming down from the Father of lights, with whom there is no variation or shifting shadow"* (James 1:17 NASB).

It should come as no surprise, then, that just as there are natural talents or gifts, there are also spiritual gifts. There is a distinction between the two. They are not the same. The topic of spiritual gifting really deserves an entire book. In fact, many books have been written on this subject with quite an array of views.

Some believe spiritual gifts are merely natural gifts that are enhanced by the Holy Spirit, while others adhere to a more literal view. That is simply to say, "spiritual" means just that: spiritual in nature. I subscribe to the latter, as my life experience and diligent study leads me to that conclusion.

God has provided many gifts that are available to all people. The free gift of salvation is one of these gifts.

For the wages of sin is death, but the gift of God is eternal life in Christ Jesus our Lord.

—Romans 6:23 KJV

For it is by grace you have been saved, through faith--and this is not from yourselves, it is the gift of God.

—Ephesians 2:8 NIV

Jesus answered, "If you knew the gift of God and who is asking you for a drink, you would have asked Him, and He would have given you living water."

—John 4:10 KJV

As each one has received a special gift, employ it in serving one another as good stewards of the manifold grace of God.

—1 Peter 4:10 NASB

We have different gifts according to the grace given us.

—Romans 12:16 KJV

In 1 Corinthians 12:1, Paul wrote: "*Now concerning spiritual gifts, brethren, I would not have you ignorant.*" The word "spiritual" in the original Greek is *pneuma*. It means "breath." Thus, we could call these breath gifts or God breathed gifts. The Greek word for "ignorant" can mean "to be unaware, to have no knowledge of, to be uninformed, to lack information, or to ignore through disinclination or willful ignorance." There are two passages in the New Testament that provide a list of these gifts: Romans 12 and 1 Corinthians 12–13. The challenge is to read these chapters without a preconceived bias as to interpretation.

I suggest you wait before reading these chapters on your own and make time to mentally prepare so that you can truly take a fresh approach with an open mind and open heart. You may also ask the Holy Spirit to help you with a fresh revelation about these gifts and how they apply to you and the church body in general. It has been a trend to view this subject as "nonessential doctrine," and as such it is often avoided. This posture could be placed into the category of willful ignorance, as listed above. I think that if the apostle Paul advised the church at Corinth to be informed, then it behooves us today to be informed, as well.

In 1 Corinthians 12:4, Paul wrote: *"Now there are varieties of gifts, but the same spirit"* (NASB). The Greek word used for "varieties" is *diairesis.* It is used to denote division, distribution, difference, and distinction. The lesson here is that the same Spirit, or one source, gives these gifts by providing *distinctiveness* to each gift.

Once a distinction is made, then there is distribution allotted by dividing it up into specific areas and usage. Anyone who has worked in a warehouse or unloaded a big truck can identify with the word picture presented here. The first part of the Greek word presents the idea of reaching out by extension. Anyone who has been involved in bread, beverage, or other grocery distribution, as I have, will identify with this part of dividing up and reaching out. We who were in that occupation would parse out to each place such as was needed. This concept in function leaves no one out, both naturally and spiritually. To each believer is given some gift. The process of discovery varies with each individual and may take time. There are some gifts that seem more visible and easier to detect than others, such as hospitality and administration. There are other gifts that seem more mysterious and even invisible, such as gifts of healing and discerning of spirits.

A common concern for most people is discovering what gifts they have. There are many ways to reveal this. One way is to consider what gifts appeal to you. What gifts in particular intrigue you? This will clue you in as to what has already been deposited into you. Growing up in a formalized religion gave me very little exposure to spiritual gifts, until I attended a meeting in which I witnessed the gift of a word of knowledge and the gifts of various healings. This experience intrigued me. I began to ask God to bring this gift into my life. I suppose I resonated with it so easily because it was already there inside of me in some fashion. It was not long afterward that I began to sense ailments in others. I would often take a step, perhaps a leap, of faith and ask the person or group of people if they had such an ailment. Many times, I would get a response and proceed to pray for that person.

That is how I discovered a genuine spiritual gift that functions through me. The apostle Paul encouraged all believers to *"earnestly desire spiritual gifts"* (1 Corinthians 14:1 NIV). The Greek word used in the original text is "zealous." To be zealous about something means to be ardent, passionate, fervent, dedicated, even fanatical. Imagine being that way about spiritual gifts!

It should be mentioned that a spiritual gift does not make you better than anyone else. Nor does it make one more spiritual or more mature than anyone else. These gifts are designed to be used with all humility and in true service to others.

The working of miracles is a gift that is rarely seen in the modern church. There are many who claim to work miracles. There are many who tell amazing stories. There are even some who may manufacture a supposed miracle for unethical reasons. Yet we know that throughout history God has indeed performed miracles.

We can recount the story of Moses and how God worked with the Jewish people for thousands of years. We have the New Testament record of Jesus performing miracles and healing thousands of people. In His earthly life, Jesus sent out the twelve disciples to perform the exact same miracles He did (Luke 9:1–6). Later Jesus sent out seventy-two disciples to heal the sick and perform miracles (Luke 10:1–17). The book of Acts records the life and events of the early church as led by the apostles. The miracles performed by the apostles are said to be numerous and astounding. All of this happened decades after Jesus died and resurrected.

I must admit that I do not know anyone who has this gift in a genuine fashion. I can say in all truth that I believe God bestowed this gift to operate through me twice in my life. Both occasions were to pray for a couple who wanted to start a family but were not able to.

I can absolutely attest to the fact that spiritual gifts are real, and despite what some Bible scholars may disseminate, they are just as valid today as they were thousands of years ago. Experience usually trumps theory in most cases, and that certainly holds true with this subject, as well.

One gift that is often misunderstood and misrepresented is the ability to speak in tongues. This is another gift I can personally attest to as real and valid. There are many factions of Christianity who believe that these gifts have ceased to exist. This is known as the doctrine of cessation. The premise of this doctrine is that when the last of the original apostles died and the church was established, there was no more need for these gifts. Although some believers have acted strange and weird concerning spiritual gifts, that does not negate the reality of a genuine expression and use of such gifts. The ability to speak in tongues is a great example of proper and improper use. The simplicity of tongues is quite overlooked. It is simply a prayer language designed to communicate with God. This language bypasses the brain. In other words, you need not think of forming words and sentences. An authentic prayer language emanates from deep within your human spirit. It need not become emotional or weird. Much like a learned language, tongues are completely in the control of the speaker's faculties. In other words, you can start and stop at any time, as well as determine your volume and pace. Those faculties of choice are still controlled by the brain; it is the words themselves, i.e., the language, that is spiritual. This phenomenon is first mentioned in the second chapter of the book of Acts. It was during the Jewish holiday of the feast of weeks, or Pentecost. The Holy Spirit fell upon the disciples as they were gathered there in an upper room. This is when and where they began to speak in tongues. This is why people who exercise this gift are often called Pentecostal believers. Terms such as *charismatic*, *Spirit-filled*, and *full Gospel* are also used to describe these expressions of the church body.

Contrary to what some Bible teachers disseminate, this gift is not from the devil. It is not foolish babble, though at times it may seem that way. It is diverse languages, known or unknown. When it happens to you, you get it. It is real. One of the most beautiful expressions of this is when a group of people begin to sing melodies in tongues and in harmony with each other. I have experienced this phenomenon numerous times, and there is simply nothing like it on earth.

The gift of discerning of spirits is designed to be used in discerning all matters spiritual. It is not the gift of suspicion. It is not the gift of fault finding and accusations. We have five natural senses, which are touch, taste, sight, hearing, and smell. Likewise, a believer can have five spiritual senses. This is a part of discerning of spirits. We can hear in the spirit. We can sense a spiritual touch. We can see in the spirit. We can also smell and taste in the spirit. I have actually experienced many of these. This ability to sense in the spirit applies to sensing God, angels, demons, and people. A genuine gift would have a balance and a mix of all. Someone who seems to be always or only sensing evil is unbalanced and incorrectly focused. The purpose of this gift, as well as all the gifts, is to help build up others and set them free. It is never to be used to destroy another person or group.

We see this demonstrated by Jesus in the book of Mark:

When Jesus saw that a crowd was running to the scene, he rebuked the impure spirit. "You deaf and mute spirit," he said, "I command you, come out of him and never enter him again."

—Mark 9:25 NIV

Jesus was able to discern that this particular demonic spirit was impure—another translation uses the word "foul"—and that this spirit was deaf and mute. Jesus cast it out, and the person was made whole.

We see the apostles in the early days of the church do much the same. Philip is one example:

Philip went down to a city in Samaria and proclaimed the Messiah there. When the crowds heard Philip and saw the signs he performed, they all paid close attention to what he said. For with shrieks, impure spirits came out of many, and many who were paralyzed or lame were healed.

—Acts 8:5–7 NIV

My own experience has taught me that basically evil spirits smell bad, while the fragrance of the presence of God may smell like roses or frankincense. I have encountered evil spirits which caused my own spirit to feel sick and oppressed as opposed to an encounter with the Holy Spirit which caused my spirit to radiate peace and joy. I am describing more than emotions. I am describing the gift of discerning of spirits.

There are some who claim to have had interaction with angels. This could be considered within the gift of discerning of spirits. I have not had such an encounter in my life as of yet. I do believe that I have sensed the presence of an angel near me at times. It is difficult to describe in words. It seems to be more of a sense or an awareness and a knowing. I have met one person who claimed to have angels appear to them in physical form and have a conversation. I can honestly say that I believe the person, because I observed the fruit of that encounter, and my spirit seemed to bear witness that it was genuine.

The gift of prophecy is one that has been misunderstood and misused ever since the early church was born. This is especially relevant today due to the nature and use of social media. Suffice it to say that anyone who claims to speak for God needs to do so in all humility. No one is infallible. We all see in part, hear in part, and prophesy in part. The gift of prophecy is primarily for encouragement, edification, and comfort (1 Corinthians 14:3). The words spoken should bear witness with the hearers and be able to pass the test of the purpose and nature of Jesus Christ as revealed in the biblical context.

There are some spiritual gifts I have not experienced. I could relate my belief as to how they work, but it would be speculative at best. It needs to be emphasized that all spiritual gifts should be wrapped in spiritual fruit. That is to say that the use and exercise of gifts needs to be done so with gentleness, kindness, patience, and the like.

13

Spiritual Fruit

I mentioned in chapter 7 the importance of spiritual fruit. I would like to take a deeper dive into this topic here. In Galatians 5:22, Paul wrote, *"The fruit of the spirit is love, joy, peace, patience, kindness, goodness, faithfulness, gentleness, self-control"* (KJV). This is the nature of spiritual fruit. It is worth noting that the Greek word here for "fruit" is *karpos*. It means fruit that is fully ripe, plucked, pulled off, taken, ready to eat. Hence, this spiritual fruit is mature. So, go over that list again and think about each one of these attributes becoming fully mature in your life. The importance of each and every one of these spiritual virtues cannot be emphasized enough. Imagine the impact this will produce with all your relationships. Imagine the impact this will produce in ministry. Imagine creating an atmosphere of peace rather than strife. What does that look like? How does that feel?

Many years ago, when I was new in the faith, I would observe ministers preaching and praying for people with great drama and emotionalism. I observed ministers exercising the gifts of the Spirit, yet not being patient, gentle, or kind with people. I learned by observation what not to do. I learned that we desperately need what I call "fruit-wrapped gifting."

The ability to wrap everything we do in spiritual fruit creates a beautiful life that others will notice. This can dramatically change the dynamics of a marriage. This can dramatically change workplace dynamics. This definitely will make church life and ministry better, if we all start to make this a daily practice. Always remember: It is a process.

One of the biggest challenges that faces most believers is the ability to live and walk in peace consistently. You would think this should be automatic, but that is not the case. We tend to think of peace as being mostly external. It is common for people to live in an atmosphere of chaos and drama. We have an amazing opportunity to live differently and bring the atmosphere of peace wherever we go. We can all start by being aware that in heaven, there is no fear, only courage. No anger, only love. No fighting and arguing, only peace. No strife, only patience and gentleness. As we go through our day, we can make an effort to be aware of what virtues are flowing through us in the moment.

Is love flowing, or is anger? Is grace flowing, or is judgment and condemnation? Is peace flowing like a river, or are we living in strife? Is stability flowing, or is chaos and self-created crisis? Objectively evaluate your life. This is a very good exercise in the life skill of awareness. The fruit we produce in our lives will be seen by others.

Okay, so how do we do this? We read in John 14:27 that Jesus said, *"Peace I give to you"* (KJV). I believe when He said that, the atmosphere changed both in His disciples and around them. In other words, they felt peaceful. There was a spiritual impartation that took place. I have experienced this impartation myself. Many times, it occurred while I was praying. One time it happened quite unexpectedly when I called a trusted minister to pray for healing. As he prayed, I was caught up into an overwhelming atmosphere of peace. What was even more surprising is that it lingered for many days. I was literally walking in peace all day and all night. From that day on, with intentional focus and practice, I was able to tap into that whenever and wherever life found me. I found new meaning and purpose when I read such verses as Romans 1:11, where the apostle Paul said, *"For I long to see you that I may impart unto you some spiritual gift to the end that you may be established"* (KJV).

This is precisely what happened with me. I soon realized there is far more to this list of spiritual fruit than meets the eye. I think most people see this list as dealing with the emotional realm. This may be true on some level, but what is most fascinating is the tangible and transformative spiritual nature of this fruit. It changed the way I carried myself. It changed the way I interacted with others and situations. It changed the way I felt and lived. I truly believe this can happen and was designed to happen with each and every fruit described.

It has been often taught that gifts are given and fruit is grown. This is largely true in the sense that even though both are spiritual, it does take time and process to grow into that which we have been called into. There is a learning curve.

We can conclude with confidence, therefore, that anyone can experience supernatural peace and love. Many people struggle with feeling loved. Love is meant to be felt and experienced. There are various reasons for this common problem. We need more than a mental assent to feel love. It is possible to experience love in full measure—spirit, soul, and body. The ability to be receptive to the full love of God is sometimes blocked by emotional and psychological trauma and/or incorrect belief systems. Nonetheless, the warmth of love from God can still flow into someone, just as water can break through rock.

I relate my story in hope that it will motivate and inspire others. My parents divorced when I was about three years of age. I often felt unloved and unwanted as I grew. I later learned that I was an unplanned pregnancy. When I met the Anointed One, He told me He loved me. When He said those words, I actually felt love. It was warm and deep. Then I felt invisible arms hug me. One cannot deny the depth of love God has and is when such an event happens. He also gave me a commission to love people. The impartation I received that day has stayed with me and compels me to become love personified. First John 1:8 tells us that *"God is love"* (NIV). God does not just have love—He is Love!

It is possible to have and live out all the spiritual fruit. When we do this and do this well, we will no longer feel a compulsion to sell the fruit of the Gospel when people can taste and see the goodness of God working through us. Perhaps the greatest expression of desirable fruit is the practice of being considerate to others. Being considerate means being polite and considering the feelings or circumstances of others. It means being respectful and helpful. This applies at home, at work, while shopping, and so on. We tend to study the Bible for knowledge, as we should, but let us also study to become fruit-wrapped gifting for others.

14

What Is the Fivefold Ministry?

The concept of the fivefold ministry is based on Ephesians 4:11–12, which reads, *"And he gave the apostles, the prophets, the evangelists, the shepherds and teachers, to equip the saints for the work of ministry, for building up the body of Christ"* (ESV).

The fivefold ministry has usually been defined as the church leadership ministry that consists of: 1) apostles, 2) prophets, 3) evangelists, 4) pastors [shepherds], and 5) teachers.

The apostle Paul wrote the letter of Ephesians about 62 AD, while he was in prison in Rome. The reason I mention this is to provide context as to the function of these gifts some thirty years after the Christian church began. There has been much debate as to whether two of these listed—apostle and prophet—have ceased to exist. It is true that within a few hundred years, the church became more institutional, with a tendency toward ritual and form. There have always been pastors and pastoral work in some form, with various titles such as elder, priest, pastor, overseer, and so on. There has always been evangelism, with some individuals being classified as evangelists. Then, of course, Bible teachers have been abundant ever since the printing press made the Bible available to everyone.

It does beg the question: If three of these gifts are currently widely accepted, then why not the other two? Most likely because of a viewpoint known as cessationism. That is, some have proposed that once the first apostles and prophets died off, these gifts were no longer needed, as the early church was well established by that point. This position lacks logic and reason. Think about it. All these gifts are from Jesus Himself and designed to build up the church body. We still view a pastor as valid. It may help us to see that Jesus embodied the fivefold ministry. Jesus is called the Good Shepherd (pastor). Jesus was a great teacher. Jesus proclaimed the kingdom of God (evangelist). He was a prophet. Jesus is called the Apostle and High Priest of our faith in Hebrews 3:1. When Jesus rose from the dead, He took of Himself and distributed these five ministry functions to individuals within His church. I would tend to think that if the gift of pastor did not cease, then neither did the other gifts.

The fivefold ministry gifts are often misunderstood and applied improperly by many leaders. There is a great tendency to see these ministries as authoritative and positions of importance. This is far from the heart and intention of Jesus. They are just what it says—gifts. I would further state them to be "grace gifts," which can never be earned.

I would classify these gifts as a function rather than a position. We are all simply members of the same body, albeit with different functions. No one member or gift or ministry is better than another. This is humility in action.

I actually have witnessed the misuse and even abuse of each of the five ministries. This is sometimes referred to as spiritual abuse. Yes, even pastors can misuse this gift. It is a consequence of patterning the church structure according to religious hierarchical traditions rather than a simple and humbler model of servant-leader. The term *pastor* is only found once in the New Testament as listed above. Other terms are used to describe a servant-leader, such as *elder*, *presbyter*, *episcopal*, and *shepherd*. For example, Philippians 1:1 states: *"To all the saints in Christ Jesus who are at Philippi, with the overseers and deacons"* (ESV). This seems to be a typical model of church leadership. Notice the plural usage: overseers (elders) and deacons. Today we often see a theater-style church, with one person who is large and in charge, namely the senior pastor. It does not appear that any New Testament writer would have supported such a model. In fact, many of the early churches functioned without a pastor at first. It appears that the people themselves were mostly self-ruled as they fellowshipped daily, met from house to house, prayed, and followed the teachings of the letters sent to them by the apostles.

We know this because of these words in the book of Acts:

When they had appointed elders for them in every church, having prayed with fasting, they commended them to the Lord in whom they had believed.
—Acts 14:23 KJV

It is worth noting that the churches existed before the elders were appointed.

For this reason I left you in Crete, that you would set in order what remains and appoint elders in every city as I directed you.
—Titus 1:15 KJV

The role of these pastors in the early church seems to be more of a facilitator and general overseer. They do not seem to be in the forefront, but rather behind the scenes caring for people. These pastors worked together as a team, along with deacons, who themselves were more like waiters for the church. The evolution of ministry from lowly servants to authoritative positions is truly most unfortunate.

The modern church structure does have benefit and has been effective in reaching the next generation. The use of technology and social media has helped in this process. Yet in doing so, we have presented a one-dimensional view of Christian life and ministry. We have created more of a "spectator" church life, when the church was designed to be an interactive and participatory experience. We do meet to worship together, and this is essential!

The main event in many church services tends to be the sermon. It seems to me that we could prioritize these two main sections of our church services differently. Our collective worship could be the main event, during which we enter into the presence of God and receive from the heavenly realm. The sermon could be condensed to be more concise, and longer sermons could be allocated to be viewed online (something we all experienced during the 2020 pandemic). Why? To make room and leave time for the benefit of experiencing other aspects of the fivefold ministry, especially those that are lacking in most church services, such as the apostolic and prophetic impartations. Why do we need these ministry gifts? A pastor tends to teach Bible stories paired with life applications. Valuable as this is, we teach what we know, but we reproduce who we are. A pastor may teach doctrine and theology, but the mentorship of a genuine apostle/prophet is designed to equip believers with elements of Christ not often seen. The problem is that many of those who claim to be apostles and prophets have no clue what that means. It is not meant to be a title someone wears. No, it never was. It was not meant to be flashy or self-promoting. It was not meant to place someone on a pedestal to be admired. These ministry gifts are to be effective in imparting supernatural life and demonstrating the reality of Jesus, while at the same time exemplifying genuine humility and self-sacrifice.

Here is how Paul describes the attributes of an apostle—listen to the humility:

For I am the least of the apostles, and not fit to be called an apostle, because I persecuted the church of God. But by the grace of God, I am what I am, and His grace toward me did not prove vain, but I labored more than all of them, yet not I but the grace of God with me.

—1 Corinthians 15:9–10 NASB

Was it a sin for me to lower myself in order to elevate you by preaching the gospel of God to you free of charge?

—2 Corinthians 11:7 NIV

In 2 Corinthians 11:23–27 (NIV), Paul is contrasting himself with others whom he called false apostles:

I am more. I have worked much harder, been in prison more frequently, been flogged more severely, and been exposed to death again and again. Five times I received from the Jews the forty lashes minus one. Three times I was beaten with rods, once I was pelted with stones, three times I was shipwrecked, I spent a night and a day in the open sea, I have been constantly on the move. I have been in danger from rivers, in danger from bandits, in danger from my fellow Jews, in danger from Gentiles; in danger in the city, in danger in the country, in danger at sea; and in danger from false believers. I have labored and toiled and have often gone without sleep; I have known hunger and thirst and have often gone without food; I have been cold and naked.

I find it most interesting to compare and contrast what we see today as apostolic ministry with the ministry of the early apostles. Times have changed, and we live in a world of technology, so naturally the methods of ministry would have a different look; however, what is noteworthy is the attitude, the humility, the character, and the gifting of the apostle Paul, as well as those whom he mentored.

The signs of a true apostle were performed among you with all perseverance, by signs and wonders and miracles.

—2 Corinthians 12:12 NASB

And I, having come unto you, brethren, came—not in superiority of discourse or wisdom—declaring to you the testimony of God, for I decided not to know anything among you, except Jesus Christ, and him crucified; and I, in weakness, and in fear, and in much trembling, was with you; and my word and my preaching was not in persuasive words of human wisdom, but in demonstration of the Spirit and of power—that your faith may not be in the wisdom of men, but in the power of God.

—1 Corinthians 2:1–5 YOUNG'S

And God wrought special miracles by the hands of Paul: So that from his body were brought unto the sick handkerchiefs or aprons, and the diseases departed from them, and the evil spirits went out of them.

—Acts 19:11–12 KJV

The life and ministry of the apostle Paul is an example of an authentic extension of the life and ministry of Jesus through an individual. It demonstrates surrender, commitment, humility, and grace. Jesus and the apostle Paul are two wonderful examples of what a minister and ministry should look like. There is such a temptation in our modern faith circles to boast about how well we know the Bible. It is clear that Paul knew the author very well. This is really the heart of fivefold ministry, as well as an organic Christian life: to know the God of the Bible so well that every virtue of Jesus is lived through us. That means demonstrating love, grace, forgiveness, healing, and yes, even miracles.

A minister who makes it all about them or money or a building or anything else is missing the mark, and perhaps even perverting what true ministry is. Authentic ministry looks like this: Compassion for all. Self-sacrificing. Not boastful. Not self-promoting. Not demanding. Not authoritative. Not condescending. But lowly and humble in a genuine and heartfelt way. Willing to listen to others. Willing to acknowledge that no one has all the answers, including the minister. Taking time to impart wisdom and not just knowledge. For example, a mechanic can learn a lot from reading a manual, but it is in the hands-on instruction where techniques are learned, and wisdom is gained. A pastor could provide hands-on nuts and bolts opportunities along with the sermon. This is called equipping the body. Genuine fivefold ministry has a feeling to it, as well. It tends to leave a deposit of something tangibly felt, yet hard to describe. It sometimes and often will cause others to have a spiritual hunger and thirst. Just because there may be differences, misunderstandings, and even confusion as to this fivefold ministry, that does not negate the benefits of the real deal, as elusive as it may be.

It seems prudent to me to address the fact that social media has given rise to many who are self-proclaimed prophets and apostles. It is stunning how gullible believers can be in following such people without question. It should be apparent when such a prophet predicts current events that never pan out as predicted that they are not the real deal. Yet it does seem to be a trend to keep following such persons and even share their videos. A social media prophet who does not admit they were incorrect in their predictions and does not humbly ask for forgiveness should raise concerns as to how they represent Jesus in our culture. God is not haphazard nor schizophrenic when He speaks. Social media can be a wonderful expression of the heart and ministry of Jesus if it is used to help others from a loving position of grace. One needs to discern the difference when following ministry on social media platforms.

15

Life Lessons About End Times

"The end is near!" a sign reads in a scene from a number of famous movies. Why the fascination with the end times, especially among Christians? Actually, this is not a new thing at all. Indeed, thousands of years ago, Jesus was asked about the end times:

And as he sat upon the mount of Olives, the disciples came unto him privately, saying, Tell us, when shall these things be? and what shall be the sign of thy coming, and of the end of the world?

—Matthew 24:3 KJV

The disciples of Jesus expected Him to overthrow Rome and set up His own political kingdom. I am sure the story of Moses played a huge part in this, as well as various passages from the prophets. When we think of the end times, we picture plagues and wars and cataclysmic events. We picture the various plagues of Egypt, with Moses being a type of Jesus. In the end, the people who love God are delivered from the evil world they once knew.

The early Christians earnestly believed they were living in the last days and that they would see the return of Jesus in what is commonly called the rapture. First Thessalonians 4:16–17 describes this event:

For the Lord himself will descend from heaven with a cry of command, with the voice of an archangel, and with the sound of the trumpet of God. And the dead in Christ will rise first. Then we who are alive, who are left, will be caught up together with them in the clouds to meet the Lord in the air, and so we will always be with the Lord. Therefore encourage one another with these words (ESV).

Also, Paul writes in 1 Corinthians 15:51–53:

Behold! I tell you a mystery. We shall not all sleep, but we shall all be changed, in a moment, in the twinkling of an eye, at the last trumpet. For the trumpet will sound, and the dead will be raised imperishable, and we shall be changed. For this perishable body must put on the imperishable, and this mortal body must put on immortality (KJV).

Many of the early believers were under the impression that the rapture had already happened and they had missed it. Paul wrote about this in 2 Thessalonians:

Now we beseech you, brethren, by the coming of our Lord Jesus Christ, and by our gathering together unto him, that ye be not soon shaken in mind, or be troubled, neither by spirit, nor by word, nor by letter as from us, as that the day of Christ is at hand. Let no man deceive you by any means: for that day shall not come, except there come a falling away first, and that man of sin be revealed, the son of perdition; Who opposeth and exalteth himself above all that is called God, or that is worshiped; so that he as God sitteth in the temple of God, shewing himself that he is God.

—2 Thessalonians 2:1–4 KJV

It seems that when there is an awareness of the words of Jesus along with the writings of the prophets, the apostle Paul, or John, who wrote the book of Revelation, there is an inclination to look for the fulfillment of these words in the world around us. Every generation, it seems, has reason to believe they are the ones to witness the end in real time. History is often neglected to be a factor in our discerning of the times. Current events are all we can see. We would be wise and do well to consider historical context when speculating about end time events.

Take, for example, Nero Julius Caesar, who was born in AD 37 and died in AD 68. He ruled during the time when most of the New Testament was being written. Nero took the throne in Rome when he was about sixteen or seventeen years old. He was afraid his stepbrother would take the throne from him, so he had him killed. There was also a power struggle for the throne between Nero and his mother, so he killed her, as well. A fire began in AD 64 that lasted nine days and

111

burned about one third of Rome. Many believed Nero set the fire himself, but he blamed the Christians and then persecuted them ruthlessly. He nailed them to crosses in his garden, and used them as human candles to light up his nights. Nero had a coin made with his image stamped on it, inscribed, "Savior of the world." It was common for Romans to ascribe divine attributes to their emperors. The family line of Caesar had titles such as "son of God" and "savior of all mankind." They would even have musicians sing these phrases in ceremonies paying homage to them. Then, there is, of course, the number "666," attributed to Nero. *Isopsephia* was a method used by the Greeks to calculate the numerical value of letters. Many have used this method to assign the number, 666, to Nero. When we combine what we know about Nero with scripture, it is no wonder the first-century church believed Nero was the "beast" (see Revelation 13:18) and that the end was near. Some scholars suspect Paul alluded to Nero when he said the mystery of iniquity is already at work (see 2 Thessalonians 2:7), although there is no way to confirm this, as Paul was not specific.

Fast-forward to 542 AD, when the bubonic plague swept through the Eastern Roman Empire, killing between twenty-five and fifty million people. One can only imagine how terrifying it must have been to live at that time. Christians would most likely have considered this to be the great tribulation (see Matthew 24:21-22). Later, around 1337, the plague erupted again, killing about one third of the population in Europe. It surfaced again in 1894 in Southeast Asia and China. About eighty thousand people died in six months.

The words of Jesus concerning wars in the end times (Matthew 24) certainly caused alarm among believers when World War I began in 1914. The Spanish flu pandemic of 1918, the deadliest in history, added to the fear of that time. This virus infected an estimated five hundred million people worldwide—about one third of the planet's population—and killed an estimated twenty to fifty million victims, including some 675,000 Americans. The 1918 flu was first observed in Europe, the United States, and parts of Asia before swiftly spreading around the world. At the time, there were no effective drugs or vaccines to treat this killer flu strain. Citizens were ordered to wear masks. Schools, theaters, and businesses were shuttered, and bodies piled up in makeshift morgues before the virus finally ended its deadly global march. Wow! Compare that to the COVID-19 pandemic of 2020. It's almost like history repeating itself. These events combined caused famine in 1918, as well. Think about how Christians would have viewed the world around them during that time. Wars, famine, and pestilence! The end must be near! Prophecies are being fulfilled! Jesus is coming back! Yet they were not correct. One could presume many pastors and other ministers preached sermons to the same theme, urging people to repent and turn to God. Some might have preached these world events as being the end time judgment from God. They did not have the full benefit of hindsight as we have today. They had some history to learn from but not the bigger picture such as we have now.

Imagine being alive not only during World War I but also World War II. Imagine seeing modern vehicles and planes and films in light of the biblical text. People were going to and fro, and knowledge was increasing (Daniel 12:4). Imagine learning about Hitler and the terrible crimes against humanity and the forced takeover of other nations. No doubt many people wondered if Hitler was the Antichrist. Christians have been playing "pin the tail on the Antichrist" ever since the days of Nero. The end is near! Prophecies are being fulfilled! Jesus is coming back? Well, no, not yet.

As time marches on, it does feel like events are speeding up. I know. I get that. We could mention smaller wars, such as the Vietnam War and the Korean War, the Gulf War, the wars in Iraq, Afghanistan, and Syria. We could mention civil wars such as what took place in Rwanda in Africa from 1990 to 1994, when approximately eight hundred thousand people were killed. We could recall deadly earthquakes, hurricanes, tsunami, floods, famines, and terrorism. All these things happening in a relatively short span of time certainly does cause it to feel like they could be end-times related. The problem is, no one really knows. We think we know, but we really do not know for sure. We might even know people who think they know. They have charts and graphs and seem to have it all figured out but…history has proven us wrong again and again.

There is a funny story from when I was young that truly illustrates this reality. I remember being about five years of age and going to the grocery store. I remember watching the workers use this thing that to me looked like a toy gun. I watched in amazement at how fast the person worked as they clicked price stickers onto every item on the shelf. I also remember when the stores made the transition to scanners and to something they called a UPC label. This method of pricing launched in June 1974 at a store in Troy, Ohio. It was not until 1982, while I was listening to a Christian radio station, that I became aware of just how sinister the UPC label was. Well, at least how sinister it was according to some. I did consider the possibility that this new technology might be used one day not to just identify and track retail items, but to track people, as well. The ministries presented it this way: According to the book of Revelation, the mark of the beast will be required in order to buy or sell. Because all retail items need a UPC code to be sold or purchased, then this must be the mark of the beast. Right?

Oh, wait—it gets better! In Revelation 13:16, the mark of the beast is to be placed on the right hand or the forehead of the person. The logical next step would be to imprint everyone on the planet with a UPC code on their forehead. Thus, we would all be given an ID number, and our information would be stored on a computer somewhere including personal history, medical history, religious beliefs, political views, and banking information. Naturally, we would be tracked by satellites as well as by the government. If we refused to take the mark (the UPC symbol), we would not be able to buy food or anything else. Okay, so needless to say, they lost me. They went too far for me. Time has proven this view did not happen as presented. The amazing part of the story is that people sold out to this idea. Churches cowered in fear. Ministries raised millions of dollars to fund the promotion to get the word out. Ministries sold end-times preparedness kits. Yes, this really happened. I witnessed it. The end is near! Prophecies are being fulfilled right in front of us in real time! Jesus is coming! Yet they were incorrect in 1982, as well. Are you beginning to see a pattern here?

Next in the advancement of society was the advent of the Internet and home computers. Needless to say, there are myriads of conspiracies concerning all of this new invasive technology. Along with this technology came the mass use of credit cards, which propelled the widespread belief that we are headed toward a one world banking system based on credit cards. In other words, the use of credit cards would cause a cashless society; hence, without the card, or the mark of the beast, no one would be able to buy or sell. Although there may be some truth in this view, it never panned out as expected.

It was during this period that a number of ministries sprang up predicting the end of the world. One of note would be Harold Camping's ministry. He was the president of Family Radio, a network of Christian radio stations based in California. He predicted the world would end on September 6, 1994. When that prediction failed to occur, he made a new calculation and said the second coming of Christ, the rapture, would happen on May 21, 2011. It has been estimated that the ministry spent a hundred million dollars in billboards and other mass media all over the world to get the message out.

Camping was mystified when the rapture did not take place in 2011. He passed away in 2013. How does this happen? How can well-meaning, devoted followers of Jesus become so obsessed, so sure of what will happen, and yet so wrong? Part of the answer can be found in taking way too much interest in world events and reading those events back into scripture with a literal view. For example, the Bible mentions in a few places that before the end takes place, the moon will appear red as blood and the sun will be dark, along with other cosmic signs (Acts 2:20). Yes, there have always been cosmic signs, and yes, some may have significance in prophecies, such as showing the Magi where Jesus was born. But not all events are the fulfillment of prophecy.

I relate a funny story concerning someone who spent thirty years studying what is called end-times biblical prophecy and eschatology. This person followed all of the respected experts in that field of study. They spent much focus on world events, especially concerning Israel, with a keen eye on the stars and the moon. The moon has many phases and sometimes is called a blue moon, an orange moon, a yellow moon, a pink moon, and a red, or blood, moon. The frequency of these events, they say, predicts the end. I listened to my fellow Christian expound on all of this with respect. I mentioned some goals I have in life and my plans for the next stage of life. He said to me, "Well, I do not think we have that long, maybe a year or so before it all winds down." That was back in 2016. It is now 2020 as I write these words, and we are still here. Humility says, "I made a mistake, I was wrong, I will not do that again." But for some reason, people who promote end-times theology never seem to admit they are wrong and will not forsake their way of thinking.

I would be amiss if I failed to mention the panic of the year 2000, or Y2K. The panic was based in a problem with the coding of computerized systems that was projected to create havoc in computer networks around the world at the beginning of the year 2000. Why? Many computers could recognize "98" as "1998" but would be unable to recognize "00" as "2000," perhaps interpreting it to mean 1900. The Y2K problem was not limited to computers running conventional software, however. Many devices containing computer chips, ranging from elevators to temperature-control systems in commercial buildings to medical equipment, were believed to be at risk, which necessitated the checking of these "embedded systems" for sensitivity to calendar dates. An estimated $300 billion was spent to upgrade computers and application programs to be Y2K-compliant (almost half of which were in the United States). As the first day of January 2000 dawned and it became apparent that computerized systems were intact, reports of relief filled the news media. These were followed by accusations that the likely incidence of failure had been greatly exaggerated from the beginning.

The Christian community viewed this as an end-times omen and suggested that the chaos would set up a one world leader to step up and solve this problem. He would be viewed as a savior of sorts. It was fully expected that planes would fall out of the sky, banks would be locked down, no one would be able to get money, and power grids would go down. No power, no water, no food, oh my! Injecting humor into the story aside, people all over the world had genuine concern and most of it was not valid.

We live with a "microwave mentality"—we expect instant results. The speed of results along with the speed in every other aspect of life seems to diminish our ability to place our current existence within a historical context. We tend to frame our lives in the now, so when "now" is gone, we look for the next "now." Life has become a series of "nows." Yesterday's news is quickly forgotten as we focus on what is happening today. This has affected the way Christians today view the end times. We see the speed of technology as it advances and it alters the way we perceive reality. We fail to frame it properly as the progression of modern life. Instead, we feel that today is much worse than ever before. Every new advancement becomes a new conspiracy. We see the evil use of technology rather than the potential for good as well. Think about it: The invention of the car, radio, television, nuclear power, satellites, computers, or anything else has the potential for either good or evil use. A balanced believer will be able to see both. We should be people who have the wisdom to be rational and reasonable while still being spiritual. This will earn us respect among diverse people and opinions.

The latest end-times technology scare has to do with cell phones and 5G technology, as well as a worldwide pandemic followed by a worldwide vaccination program. I am not attempting to make light of these things. I realize the absolute seriousness of all of the above. However, the extent of the conspiracies that well-meaning Christians hold is irrational and borders on paranoia.

Cell phones use a wireless signal sent through a series of cell towers. The signal has gone through many innovations, from an LTE signal to 2G, then 3G, then 4G, and now 5G. All that means is "next generation." Each generation has better and faster signals used for download speeds and reducing annoying lag. How, then, does this normal progression of life and technology connect with a pandemic? Well, it starts with creating a virus that is released into the general population. At the same time, the 5G network is being set into place worldwide. Also, at the same time a vaccine for the newly man-made virus is being created. This vaccine will be mass-produced to the level that everyone on the planet can be vaccinated. That is over seven billion people.

The ability to make a microchip that is implanted under the skin has already been achieved, and such microchips are already in use at this time. The newer versions of this microchip, they say, will be small enough to fit into a hypodermic needle while containing certain information and have the ability to connect to a cell or wi-fi signal. The "evil plan" is executed when the entire population is vaccinated and secretly given the microchip through the vaccine. Once this is accomplished, the leaders of the new world order or one world government will use the 5G network to connect to every human on the planet and turn them into zombies who will do whatever they are commanded through computer programming.

Does this sound rational or irrational? It is stunning how many people believe this will actually happen. Perhaps it is because some have a tendency to connect dots that really are not connected. It certainly is plausible, considering the involvement of billionaires who are interested in gaining power through wealth. Power and control do often go together. Or perhaps we are caught in wishful hopes that we will be the generation to see it all happen—to experience the rapture! Well, perhaps not yet.

The best advice I can offer is for you to live each day to your best ability without distraction as to end-times obsession. It is good to have some knowledge on the subject, as long as you are not spending all your time and energy on it. A far better use of your time and energy is to help others in practical ways and be a stabilizing factor in your sphere of influence.

16

In It, Not of It: Navigating the World Around Us

Life seems so busy and chaotic at times. We often experience information overload. Life can be full of stress. There seems to be too much to do and not enough hours to do it all. We are bombarded with sounds and images that distract us, confuse us, enrage us, or worse yet, cause us to obsess. These external inputs may cause sensory overload. Life feels complicated, and the problems seem so complex. We long for simpler times. We long for peace. We feel lost and overwhelmed. We feel anxiety, and some even feel hopeless and depressed, like a ship tossed at sea. How do we navigate such waters?

In the world, but not of it is a concise phrase we use to summarize some of what Jesus taught. For example, He spoke these words in the book of John:

"I have given them Your word; and the world has hated them, because they are not of the world, even as I am not of the world. I do not ask You to take them out of the world, but to keep them from the evil one. They are not of the world, even as I am not of the world."

—John 17:14–16 NASB

The illustration of a ship at sea is a fairly good one to express our journey through life. We have a destination with a set course. There may be unexpected events that occur that may delay us or steer us off course a bit. We are the captain of our ship, and it is our responsibility to readjust and stay the course. We learn as we go and gain skill by experience. The trick, of course, is not to let water get into the ship and overwhelm it. We are the ship, in a sense, and the water is the world around us. We are in the water, but not of it. The water is there as a vehicle of transport that we must navigate. To turn around and head back to shore because we think the journey is too difficult is to miss the mark.

The term "the world" refers to the corrupt systems of the world. The world's system is based on pride, arrogance, deceit, hatred, stealing, cheating, power, lies, abusiveness, anger, resentment, unforgiving, greed, and selfishness, to name a few.

We are in this world, but we do not need to conform to these lower attributes of the mind and behavior. Jesus said the believer ought to be a light in the darkness and salt in the earth. We have all been exposed to unhealthy environments, which contributes to our emotional and psychological development. Some of us grew up in a dysfunctional family. Some of us grew up in an abusive family atmosphere. Some of us experienced these environments later in life. Either way, the corrupt system finds a way into our life, much like a virus attacks the body or a computer. The apostle Paul encouraged Christians to be transformed by the renewing of the mind (Romans 12:2). Much like a computer, we can remove the old program and replace it with a better one. This requires time, effort, and intention.

Once we do this, it becomes easier to be surrounded by a corrupt system without it affecting us. Yet, even so, some Christians feel awkward, timid, and fearful when relating to others who have not been transformed in their own lives. Anxiety is often felt, and the urge to get away and hide from the world becomes a habit. This is far from our identity in Christ.

Let's consider how Jesus interacted with the world around Him and use that to take away some practical concepts that will help us be better ambassadors for Him. Jesus made it clear that there are two kingdoms and that His kingdom is not of this world (John 18:36). Yet we find Jesus attending weddings and other social gatherings. It should be noted that in that day and culture, such events would happen over a period of days. These were extended celebrations with food, dancing, wine, and much conversation. In fact, Jesus was accused of hanging out with the worst of society (Luke 7:34). Some may think, *Well, that was Jesus. Of course He could do that and not be affected.* The principle that enables us to encounter any situation truly comes down to how we identify with light and love. Light always displaces darkness. It is never the other way around. When you remove the light from the situation, darkness is still there, but the light is still the light. It is constant and consistent. This is the key to overcoming the world system that surrounds us. We must practice being a constant and consistent light that never dims. We do this by choosing our identity in Him and not in ourselves or our own self-effort.

It is not that we should purposely seek out dark and seedy places. It is that when we go to work, shop, dine, vacation, or just live in a neighborhood, we are not afraid or timid to be there and we become the hands of Jesus to others. We do not have to preach at people in order to be this light. We need to love people and be there as a stabilizing force. We should be slow to speak and quick to listen, slow to judge and quick to show compassion and empathy. Just like light displaces darkness, perfect love displaces fear. You might recall how many times Jesus said, "Fear not." Why? Fear is a negative emotion. Fear is simply having faith in the wrong thing. In fact, the entire world system leans toward the negative. Much like the force of gravity, the pull of the negative seems to be the dominant way of the world. It takes tremendous thrust to escape the gravitational pull of the earth. Likewise, it takes an intentional and determined thrust of faith to escape the negative pull of the world and its corrupt systems. The results of consistent practice of escaping negative forces will become very evident to us and those we encounter.

Others will take notice that something is different about you and me. They will notice that we navigate life well. It all begins with what we focus on: the good or the evil? We get to choose.

One of the better ways to navigate and interact with others is to stop talking *at* people and start talking *with* them. In other words, engage in a *two-way* conversation. I have had so many encounters with people who were so interested in getting out their talking points that it left no room for my response. Some even double down and refuse to listen if you dare to disagree. I have noticed that people who do this as a habit appear to be thinking about the next thing they are going to say instead of truly hearing the other person. It is like they are talking to hear themselves talk. This kind of person may be narcissistic. If you do not know what that term means, please look it up. This personality type tends to be self-absorbed, selfish, and manipulative. We should all examine our own behavior to avoid being a narcissist. If we have this disorder, we should seek help to resolve those issues because it will make us a better person and help us to better navigate life as well.

Here is something that will make a profound difference in your life. Are you ready? Here it is: Stop being judgmental! The dictionary defines *judgmental* as being quick to criticize, feeling morally superior, and having or displaying an excessively critical point of view. When we are judgmental, we are critically nitpicking and finding fault with another person, group of people, idea, or situation. This often causes a person to feel angry, and sometimes they are not even sure why they feel that way. To build relationships and a good reputation we need to work on rooting judgmentalism out of our lives. The alternative path we can take is to learn to practice grace. Too often, when someone is judgmental, it leads to strife and arguments, which tears apart relationships. I mentioned avoiding strife in chapter 5. It would be worth taking a look at this again and applying it to this lesson. The results you will see when this shift in paradigms is made will be amazing. Life becomes much easier and smoother when a new mind-set is adopted. You own it! You get it! And everyone will take notice. There was a nationwide fitness chain that used the motto: "Judgment-free zone." We can adopt this motto and apply it to the lives we live and the places we go.

One of the best tools for navigating the world around us is a skill known as being present. Most of our time is spent in the past or the future, rather than in the present moment. What we end up doing is passing through that moment on the way to somewhere else, and in doing so, we miss the current moment. That's how life ends up passing us by—we do it to ourselves. Being present is an act of awareness. Some may call it focus, but either way it is paying attention to the *now*. Paying attention to what you are doing right now at the moment. Paying attention to how you feel and to your own body language. Paying attention to what is happening around you. Paying attention to what someone else is saying without being distracted. Paying attention to how they feel and act. The problem is, we are not always the best indicator as to how present we actually are. It is other people who can validate whether we are being present or not. For example, have you ever had a conversation and moments later had no clue what the other person just said? Likewise, we can talk to others and somewhere in the conversation pause and ask, "Are you even listening?" What do we mean? We are saying that the other person is not present. This can cause great misunderstandings.

Many problems in life can be resolved or altogether avoided by the art of being present. We do this by placing more value on what the other person wants than on what we want. The art of listening, therefore, becomes wanting to hear more than wanting to speak. It is to focus less on yourself and more on others. This requires us to be less needy. Most people do not like to be around someone who is always needy. We can serve others by meeting their needs with delight and a positive attitude. Listening attentively is meeting a need, yet our attitude in doing so is quite important. Attitude is everything. Service to others means sacrificing your interests for the good of others. We gladly go the extra mile to be helpful. This also includes being considerate and polite to everyone and in all situations, as mentioned in chapter 13. There is a famous saying that says, "People may not always remember what you said, but they will remember how you made them feel." When we incorporate all these ingredients into our daily life, it makes us feel better and nourishes everything around us to make it better.

No matter how much water is in the ocean, it need not get into our ship. This is the key. Most people in the world do not see a problem with not keeping their word. It is okay with them. No one is perfect, they say. Everyone lies once in a while, they say. I find that many people lack integrity. Integrity means my words and my actions should always line up. Integrity means you can place your absolute trust in it. There are times when it seems difficult to follow through on something. That is when we need to do it anyway, no matter how we feel. Why? Because we said we were going to do it, and that settles it. I gave my word and I keep my word, no matter what. That is integrity. When we become decisively decisive to live this way, it creates a brand-new paradigm and leads us into a life of strength and stability. Living a life filled with integrity prevents self-made crises and chaos from happening. Living this way in every area of life with everyone we meet builds trust and confidence, the foundation of relationships. It is surely living life in the world but not being of it. It is definitely swimming upstream from the flow of the world's current.

A final thought is to avoid the trap of blaming everything bad that happens on the devil. We do live in a fallen world, and sometimes life just happens. It rains on the just and the unjust (Matthew 5:45). People make mistakes, cars break down, electronics fail, our bodies get rundown and sometimes sick, relatives argue, flights get delayed, weather happens, and so on. That is not to ignore that there is, indeed, a spiritual world, because there is one. I have experienced this world in many ways. I have had heavenly encounters that made me long for more and await heaven with great anticipation. I have also encountered dark forces that made it clear to me that evil exists and that what is invisible is just as real as the physical. There are angelic beings, and there are demonic beings. What we focus on the most tends to expand in our world the most. When we assign a spiritual cause to a natural problem, we have lost our footing, so to speak. We ought to be aware of spiritual events but so well grounded that we are balanced in our mind and emotions to the extent that we are never moved by what is happening to us. In other words, we have our heads in the right place and we are as cool as cucumbers. Yes, we can be in the world and yet be truly not of it. Set sail! Stay the course! Be confident that God is with you!

17

One Body

The human body is an amazing machine that has intricate systems working together seemingly without effort. The heart will beat about three billion times in an average lifespan. It beats about a hundred thousand times per day and sends two thousand gallons of blood through your system each day. During an average lifetime, the heart will pump nearly 1.5 million barrels of blood—enough to fill two hundred train tank cars. Your blood vessels, if laid end to end, would measure more than sixty thousand miles. That would circle the earth four times. The average adult takes about twenty thousand breaths a day. The human body is comprised of the circulatory, digestive, endocrine, immune, lymphatic, nervous, muscular, reproductive, skeletal, and respiratory systems, and they all work together in coordination.

The church is compared to the human body: *"Now ye are the body of Christ, and members in particular"* (1 Corinthians 12:27 KJV). To be healthy, it also needs to work together.

Here is most of the entire chapter, 1 Corinthians 12:12–27 (KJV):

For as the body is one, and hath many members, and all

the members of that one body, being many, are one body: so also is Christ. For by one Spirit are we all baptized into one body, whether we be Jews or Gentiles, whether we be bond or free; and have been all made to drink into one Spirit. For the body is not one member, but many. If the foot shall say, Because I am not the hand, I am not of the body; is it therefore not of the body? And if the ear shall say, Because I am not the eye, I am not of the body; is it therefore not of the body? If the whole body were an eye, where were the hearing? If the whole were hearing, where were the smelling? But now hath God set the members every one of them in the body, as it hath pleased him. And if they were all one member, where were the body? But now are they many members, yet but one body. And the eye cannot say unto the hand, I have no need of thee: nor again the head to the feet, I have no need of you. Nay, much more those members of the body, which seem to be more feeble, are necessary: And those members of the body, which we think to be less honourable, upon these we bestow more abundant honour; and our uncomely parts have more abundant comeliness. For our comely parts have no need: but God hath tempered the body together, having given more abundant honour to that part which lacked: That there should be no schism in the body; but that the members should have the same care one for another. And whether one member suffer, all the members suffer with it; or one member be honoured, all the members rejoice with it. Now ye are the body of Christ, and members in particular.

The practical application here is profound. There are perhaps billions of professing Christians all around the world. They are diverse in their ethnicity, culture, denominations, and doctrinal beliefs. Yet they (we) are one body of believers. This is highly significant and should be placed very high in what we value. There is a tendency among Christians to have somewhat of a pack mentality. We tend to run with those with whom we agree and look down on those who are not in agreement with us. We sometimes act as if we have the corner on truth. We may even feel like God is with us or favors our group more than another. These attitudes are the antithesis of an organic Christian life.

We allow there to be factions and divisions in the church body, even to the point of refusing to work alongside others. This is an unhealthy view of the global church body. When the apostle Paul used the word *schism*, it means a split, or tear, as in a fabric. In other words, although the church body has different styles of expression, our unity should be seamless. This is not an easy task. To do this requires a commitment and willingness to give up our self-imposed right to always be right. Unity does not always mean uniformity. Unity does not mean absolute conformity. These two aforementioned traits are often the foundations of cultlike organizations. Seamless unity means we accept that we do not have the corner on all truth and that other views should not prevent us from fellowship with those with whom we may differ. We may disagree on some things, but we need not be disagreeable in our behavior.

But if you bite and devour one another [in bickering and strife], watch out that you [along with your entire fellowship] are not consumed by one another.
—Galatians 5:15 AMP

The Passion Translation reads like this: *"But if you continue to criticize and come against each other over minor issues, you're acting like wild beasts trying to destroy one another!"*

Picture yourself biting and eating your own hand. Silly and gross right? Yet when you picture the global church body, with all of the numerous denominations and widely diverse local expressions, we do tend to gnaw at our own body parts. This is a really bad habit, and we need to stop it! It is alarming how many so-called ministries that use social media devote the entire ministry on criticizing everyone else. It is as if they are out to prove that everyone else is wrong and in error. Yet they cannot see the hypocrisy in doing so. We should be better than this. Let us be very attentive not to lower ourselves to such mind-sets.

In Ephesians 4:13, Paul wrote: *"until we all attain to the unity of the faith, and of the knowledge of the Son of God, to a mature man, to the measure of the stature which belongs to the fullness of Christ"* (NASB). The "until" in this verse refers to why and how long we are to benefit from the fivefold ministry.

Notice this inspired instruction did not say "until we have

unity of doctrine," but "unity of faith." We are to become mature and not act like children. We do not have the luxury of acting like we do not need another part of the body. It is not us versus them. Those who hold different views are not our enemies; they are, in a very real sense, part of us. I have enjoyed going to a wide variety of church services. Some were too boring for me, some were too long, some were too weird and bizarre, some were exciting and made me feel ten feet tall, but the greatest of all were the people I met, the beloved of God! People of every color, background, age, and strongly held beliefs. The only thing that mattered is that, for those moments in time, we were one body in Christ. All other factors disappeared, as they ought to. This is where we start and finish: one faith and one body.

We have a tendency to focus on methodology as a litmus test for what we consider to be the legitimate Christian church life. Yet the beauty of the body is that we are all different and we each have a unique function. Some may fall into the trap of comparing churches or even other believers to themselves. At first, it seems righteous to ask why someone does not express their faith exactly as we do, but this can quickly decline into a critical and judgmental attitude. This creates unreal expectations of others to conform to our way of speaking, living, acting, and posting on social media. When others do not meet our expectations, we may begin to classify them as not a part of the true church body. In other words, our perception is that we are being obedient to God and they are not. This kind of attitude is not rightly discerning the body, and it is causing the body to be divided.

The apostle Paul spoke about it even at the early stages of the church. He asked Christians why they fell into camps. One group said they were with Paul; another group said they were with Peter.

In 1 Corinthians 1:10–13 (KJV), Paul wrote:

Now I beseech you, brethren, by the name of our Lord Jesus Christ, that ye all speak the same thing, and that there be no divisions among you; but that ye be perfectly joined together in the same mind and in the same judgment. For it hath been declared unto me of you, my brethren, by them which are of the house of Chloe, that there are contentions among you. Now this I say, that every one of you saith, I am of Paul; and I of Apollos; and I of Cephas; and I of Christ. Is Christ divided? was Paul crucified for you? or were ye baptized in the name of Paul?" So, Paul presented the question, "Is Christ divided?" No, of course not…and neither should we be!

We need to resist the habit of placing people into categories. God loves people. Jesus died for everyone. Not only is every believer a child of God through creation and adoption, but every nonbeliever was created to be adopted into the family of God. Too often, Christians present an attitude of "us versus them" in terms of the world. I think we get confused in our definitions. The "world" can mean all people and living creatures, but the "world" can also mean a corrupt world system. We are instructed to avoid the traps of the world system, yet we are encouraged to love the creation, including all people whom Jesus would pursue with passionate love and compassionate grace. We are one race with great diversity. We do belong together.

I liken it to a giant jigsaw puzzle with billions of pieces. Many pieces are missing. It is our mission to seek out and find those people—those who are outside the frame, as it were. It is up to the Holy Spirit to place the pieces as He sees fit. Our role is to be humble, patient, faithful vessels of the grace life that flows from heaven.

We should avoid accusing others of being lukewarm in their faith. God is the judge of all, not us. We need to avoid taking the temperature of others. Given the choice of being a thermometer or a thermostat, let us choose to be a thermostat and lovingly warm others with kindness and gentleness. Let us consider that we are all unique and we ought not expect others to be exactly like us. We need to be considerate and not project unreal expectations onto others. We are all at various stages of life and of faith. We all have some baggage from our past that needs healing.

18

Who Are You?

A popular song from 1978 by the rock band The Who was titled "Who Are You?" The 1987 movie *The Princess Bride* has many famous quotes, and one of them was spoken by the character Inigo Montoya, who asked, "Who are you? I must know." There seems to be an identity crisis in our world today, more so now than ever before. It has become the norm to believe that what you are, what you do, and what you associate with is the same as your identity. I think it is far more important to discover and know *who* you are rather than *what* you are. This should resonate with people of faith because our identity has eternal significance.

You Are Redeemed

"Or do you not know that your bodies are a sanctuary of the Holy Spirit who is within you—the Spirit whom you have from God? And you are not your own, for you have been redeemed at infinite cost. Therefore glorify God in your bodies," the apostle Paul wrote in 1 Corinthians 6:19–20

(WEYMOUTH). I can think of a few illustrations that unpack this concept. The first is when someone purchases a house. The property has a new owner who paid a price for it. The new owner will often remodel or redecorate the house in order to customize it.

God is like that. He purchased us, and He then begins the process of making us over to what He likes. He makes us His dwelling place. Who are we? Well, we are not our own, and that is a good thing because we should desire to be a dwelling place for God.

For you have died and your life is hidden with Christ in God.

—Colossians 3:3 NASB

We typically quote this in reference to water baptism, and rightly so, because it is a beautiful visual portrait of a spiritual reality. I talked about this mystery in chapter 1, that is, Christ in you, the hope of glory. So, we truly are God's house, both corporately and as individuals. We should take time to really ponder and grasp this concept. It will reshape our view as to who we are. It will produce tremendous security and the sense that we are part of something bigger than ourselves.

The psalmist wrote these beautiful words:

O give thanks unto the LORD, *for he is good: for his mercy endureth forever. Let the redeemed of the* LORD *say so, whom he hath redeemed from the hand of the enemy.*

—Psalm 107:1–2 KJV

You are redeemed! What does that mean, exactly? The dictionary defines *redeemed* this way: gain or regain possession of (something) in exchange for payment. Also, to recover ownership of by paying a specified sum: *redeemed the ring from the pawnbroker,* for example. In terms of faith, it means we have been transferred from darkness and into light.

It is God who has delivered us out of the dominion of darkness, and has transferred us into the Kingdom of His dearly-loved Son.

—Colossians 1:3 WEYMOUTH

This is redemption. We should, therefore, have bold confidence as to where we stand and how we stand in the sight of God. We belong to a different world, a different kingdom. We belong to God. In a very true sense, you are His, and He is yours. Today, no matter how you feel, this is a truth to be owned. We should always do our best to meet and exceed expectations, yet even if we fail, this truth remains the same. We belong to Somebody who places value on us.

You Are Salt

Who are you? Jesus said: *"You are the salt of the earth. But if the salt loses its saltiness, how can it be made salty again? It is no longer good for anything, except to be thrown out and trampled underfoot"* (Matthew 5:13 KJV).

How do we use salt? We sprinkle it on our food. The food

does not flavor the salt; it is the salt that flavors the meal. We would not pour the salt into a mound at the corner of our plate. That would be absurd! Yet we tend to think of church in this way. We all gather together in one corner. To go to church is fine as long as we are being the church as we go on our way to flavor the world around us with the taste of heaven. Too often Christians are afraid of being contaminated by the world around them, and therefore they become ineffective in salting the earth. I find enjoyment as I walk through my day in knowing I am sprinkling salt as I walk. Think about that word picture. You are salt. You walk, you salt. You walk, you salt. Everywhere you go, and in everything you do, picture salt flowing out of you.

You Are Spirit, Soul, and Body

You are spirit, soul, and body. This one truth alone can change the way you think about yourself. For some, it may be a complete paradigm shift to think this way. In 1 Thessalonians 5:23, Paul wrote: *"And the God of peace himself sanctify you wholly; and may your spirit and soul and body be preserved entire, without blame at the coming of our Lord Jesus Christ"* (ERV).

The moment you were born from above, or born again, is the very moment the Holy Spirit became one with your spirit and made it alive! You were spiritually born! Yet your soul and your body remained the same. This is where the real work of transformation becomes our responsibility. It has been said that we are a spirit, we have a soul, and we live in a body. Our body is our earth suit. We need it to live here on planet earth. We should exert all due diligence to take care of it properly. That means what we eat should be healthy, we should keep our weight within reason by diet and exercise, and we should take advantage of any supplements that are safe and effective.

Our soul is where the human will resides. Our will determines our power to decide. Our soul also is comprised of the spectrum of emotions, be they good or bad. Our soul is also the realm of our mind or thought life. I like to think of it this way: Our brain is the hardware of this human computer, and the mind is the software. Most of us, if not all of us, have software programmed into us that has problems or bugs as they are known. As we age, many of us experience various forms of trauma that cause viruses to infiltrate our minds, thus causing disruption and dysfunction in our thought lives and our emotional lives, i.e., our soul.

We must, therefore, know who we are and how to distinguish between soul, spirit, and body, so we can experience real growth and progress as we better mirror the image of the One who saved us, Jesus Christ.

Our thought life is so important because it is the place where failure or success is determined. It is a circle of life, in a sense. What we think determines largely how we feel emotionally. How we feel emotionally often determines how we act or behave. How we act determines the consequences in our lives, be they good or bad. Also, how we feel often determines what we say and how we say it. Words also have consequences, be they spoken or written on social media. The bottom line is, it all starts with the thoughts we think. Our lives, in many ways, become what we think about.

This is where our will plays a big part. We can choose what to think. We really can! I like to keep it simple and easy, so I place my thoughts into files or categories. Is a thought good or bad? Is it positive or negative? Is it helping me or hurting me? Is it helping someone else or hurting them? I might also add to the list, is this how God thinks about me? Then I process the thoughts and determine if this is who I really am or, in other words, does it reflect the identity God has placed into my spirit? If not, I reject those thoughts and refuse to accept them. I say out loud to myself, "That is not me, that is not who I am, and I reject these thoughts. These thoughts stem from darkness or what my past has projected onto me. I refuse any garbage thoughts and feelings that someone or something else has placed on me."

I know this takes effort and energy and discipline, but over time, it will be a very effective tool in discovering the person God has already made you, the person you will grow into.

Casting down imaginations, and every high thing that exalteth itself against the knowledge of God, and bringing into captivity every thought to the obedience of Christ.

—2 Corinthians 10:5 KJV

Here we see that our thoughts are described as "imaginations." God has placed in everyone the capacity for imagination. We can have good ones or what I refer to as false imaginations. We therefore bring these false thoughts into captivity one by one. We may need to slow down our brain in order to do this, much like driving a car around a tight curve, we need to slow down to maintain proper control and balance. This is a good principle, a God principle. It also helps us to relate to others as we gain insight into what makes someone act the way they do. We can exercise patience, kindness, and gentleness with others because we know we also have to develop this life skill. Perhaps then we will help someone else in the process and share our faith with others.

You, the true you, are not only your body or your soul, but you are also your spirit. As far as God is concerned, you are a spirit form. This is highly significant because as a spirit you are alive forever. You are an eternal being. When we pass away, we simply walk from earth into heaven, much like you would walk from one room into another room at your place of work or in your home. When we become spirit-minded, our perspective changes. We see the world around us as temporary. We are merely travelers on a journey.

In John 4:24, Jesus said, *"God is a Spirit: and they that worship him must worship him in spirit and in truth"* (KJV).

You are primarily a spirit, and that is the primary way we connect to God. It is our Wi-Fi connection. To be spirit-minded is easier than it seems. It means that as we walk through our day, we can actively be in an atmosphere of worship all day no matter what we are doing because we are a spirit. It is a matter of focus and awareness. In other words, worship can be a physical act, such as singing in church or in a car, but it can also be a simple expression from the heart connected by the spirit. One may worship in spirit during any activity! You can worship with your spirit and your soul and your body! All because Jesus opened the door. In fact, He is the door.

You are the beloved of God and fully accepted by Him!

To all who are beloved of God in Rome, called as saints: Grace to you and peace from God our Father and the Lord Jesus Christ.

—Romans 1:7 NASB

I write this letter to all his beloved chosen ones in Rome, for you have been divinely summoned to be holy. May his joyous grace and total well-being, flowing from our Father and the Lord Jesus Christ, rest upon you.

—Romans 1:7 TPT

Put on therefore, as the elect of God, holy and beloved, bowels of mercies, kindness, humbleness of mind, meekness, longsuffering.

—Colossians 3:12 KJV

To the praise of the glory of his grace, wherein he hath made us accepted in the beloved.

—Ephesians 1:6 KJV

For it was always in his perfect plan to adopt us as his delightful children, through our union with Jesus, the Anointed One, so that his tremendous love that cascades over us would glorify his grace—for the same love he has for his Beloved One, Jesus, he has for us. And this unfolding plan brings him great pleasure!

—Ephesians 1:6 TPT

The word "beloved" is a term used to describe a special affection. For example, when a couple join in marriage, they may call each other "my beloved." In the biblical sense, we are dearly beloved children of God. It is much like a woman who gives birth and looks at her child with adoring affection and deep love because this child came from her. Likewise, God has summoned or called us to be born of the Spirit, so we are part of Him. We are the beloved born ones of God.

To know we are loved is one of the most amazing facets of life we have. The key is to translate that from the intellect to the heart, into love that is deeply experienced in such a way that it can never be stolen. This produces a sense of security unlike anything else. When we are secure in this love, the circumstances of our environment will not move us. We know that we know that we know we are living and moving in an atmosphere of love from above. Love becomes our constant state of being, just like God, who is love.

19

It's Going to Take Faith

"It did not go quite as you planned, you are asking what it will take, it's going to take faith." These are lyrics to a song written by Gary Tash. The song made quite an impression on me in my youth and provided inspiration as well as motivation.

In fact, in very real terms, living an organic Christian life is a life of *faith*! "We walk by faith and not by sight" is a phrase from one of my favorite verses from the Bible (2 Corinthians 5:7). This one verse has profoundly affected how I managed to stay strong and stable while enduring difficult times and seasons. Simply stated, faith is trust. Faith is peace and confidence. Faith is always hopeful and positive. Fear has worry and anxiety. Fear is simply having faith in the wrong thing. To walk by faith and not by sight means that I keep walking in a straight path going forward, no matter what happens around me. The outside world does not define who I am, who God is, how I live, nor how I feel. My five physical senses are how I contact this physical world, yet they need not make me feel unsteady in my spiritual walk and push me around. A good way to understand this is to realize we do not have to be moved by what we see, what we hear, how we feel, or what others say or do. We walk and do not stumble despite what is happening around us. We remain constant and consistent in our walk because God Himself, the Author of our faith, is constant and consistent. We know what we believe and in whom we believe. We know there is much more to life than what we can see with our physical eyes. Many accomplishments happened in life when people used the eye of faith to see the yet unseen become a reality.

Now faith is the substance of things hoped for, the evidence of things not seen.

—Hebrews 11:1 KJV

Living a life of genuine faith is most assuredly a challenge. It often requires tenacity, patience, vision, long-term thinking, and daring to be different while staying humble. Rest assured the rewards in doing so are like finding gold.

The subject of faith is well worth investing time and study. Jesus talked about faith a lot. He mentioned having great faith, no faith, short faith, and little faith, and He compared faith to a tiny seed. The apostles Paul, Peter, and John all mentioned faith in their various epistles to the churches. They use phrases such as "ever-increasing faith," "faith and patience," "faith works by love," "faith that grows," "generational faith," "enduring faith," "justified by faith," "the good fight of faith," "the shield of faith," "faith as a grace gift," and many more. The subject is certainly a treasure chest of infinite value to anyone who will spend the time and expend the energy to learn it well. I have been in the faith for over 40 years now. I have found great satisfaction in the practice of faith that endures. I would recommend the same for anyone. I have seen believers who seem to have barely any problems in life and I have seen believers who faced overwhelming difficulties, yet the one thing that defines each is when we have faith that endures.

20

Happy Birthday!

Every one of us was born into this world. Our birthday is often a time of celebration—and, of course, cake. What most people in this world do not know is that a natural birth will have an end of life, but a spiritual birth has no end and lasts forever! There is a natural birth, and there is a spiritual birth. Both are real! Some may call the latter a new birth, born from above, a rebirth, or born again. No matter what term is applied, it is a valid experience available to anyone and everyone.

In John 3:5–7, Jesus said, "*I tell you the truth, no one can enter the kingdom of God unless he is born of water and the Spirit. Flesh gives birth to flesh, but the Spirit gives birth to spirit. You should not be surprised at my saying, 'You must be born again'*" (NIV).

So, we see where the term "born again" came from. Jesus was communicating a completely new concept about heaven. He made it so simple. To enter earth, all that is needed is a birth. To enter heaven, all that is needed is a spiritual birth.

Think about how profound that is! Once you are born into this earth, is it possible to be unborn? Likewise, once you are born again by a spiritual birth, you cannot be unborn spiritually! You will always be a child of God! Always! It does not get any more organic than this. If you have never experienced a new birth, this is your invitation! Your parents gave you biological life. Jesus gives you spiritual life by your act of simple and humble surrender to His divine forgiveness and grace. Jesus gave His life, and He desires to be your personal Savior! Yes, Lord! Please forgive me, cleanse me, and be my closest companion. Not only will you be sure you will enter heaven, but now heaven will live inside you by His Spirit.

Conclusion

It has been said of a professing Christian that they may be the only Bible someone may read. So, what is a Christian? What does that look like? How should a Christian make someone feel when they are encountered?

When I met the Anointed One, Jesus, the atmosphere was so distinct that there could be no doubt as to who was there. There is only one Jesus. To be a genuine Christian means that we carry the very same atmosphere with us, or to be exact, Christ inside of us. Anyone can grasp this even if they do not have biblical knowledge or any theological doctrinal beliefs.

Organic Christian life begins as a seed and continues to grow as we ensure we are properly nourished.

For you have been born again not of seed which is perishable but imperishable, that is, through the living and enduring word of God.
                                                        —1 Peter 1:23 NASB

This seed is unlike any other, for it is a spiritual seed. It is pure and eternal! The soil it is planted in may be natural—that soil being us—but this is where the miracle begins.

Good Ground Family Church is the name of a local church near where I grew up. I love that name, as it describes so well what organic faith takes: good ground. In Mark 4, Jesus talked about the kingdom of heaven being like a seed that is planted in soil. The seed planted in the good soil produced thirty-, sixty-, and even a one-hundred-fold return on the harvest. Good ground is the organic soil of our heart and minds that is not tainted by religious thought, traditions, nor anything else that would contaminate the simplicity and purity of the Gospel. The incorruptible seed that is in you will continue to grow with no end as you provide plenty of sunshine, spiritual water, and weeding to the garden. This takes time and effort. Deep, deep roots are vital to this process. The goal is to grow into a beautiful tree that bears much fruit. Others then can partake of this spiritual fruit, and the seed is planted in them and reproduces Christ in them over and over again. The Tree of Life becomes an orchard of trees.

We have a need to unlearn some common concepts. Take, for example, the Garden of Eden. There were two unique trees: the Tree of Life and the Tree of the Knowledge of Good and Evil. God told Adam and Eve not to partake of the Tree of the Knowledge of Good and Evil, as the story relates. Jesus demonstrated the difference between these two ways of living with His teaching, His miracles, and His way of life. Yet, for thousands of years since then, most Christians attempt to live by and through the wrong tree. We tend to focus on *what* we are doing right and *what* we are doing wrong. We measure our Christian walk by how well we follow the good and forsake the evil. We measure our progress by comparing it with others. We focus on sin—the sins of commission and the sins of omission. We are taught to do this and not to do that. In other words, we define our life, faith, and spiritual walk by our use of the Tree of the Knowledge of Good and Evil. We were designed to exist by and through the Tree of Life. We ought to define our life, faith, and walk by how we are becoming one with the very life of God. This is a lesson very few believers grasp, let alone incorporate in practical ways. We were designed to walk with God by relational learning even more than academic learning.

May you dare to be the one who embraces it, learns it, lives it, and demonstrates it to others. I would be remiss not to mention that we should strive always to do the right thing while we go through our days, weeks, months, and years. To live by sound principles is a part of this life of faith. The following is a list of sound practical advice:

- Be teachable.

- Be gentle and patient with everyone.

- Talk to others without an agenda.

- Some plant the seed, some water, and some harvest.

- Run the race with patience. It is a marathon.

- Grace is not just a subject; it is a lifestyle. Have grace for yourself and for others.

- Faith is not just a subject; it is also a lifestyle.

- Forgive yourself, then forgive others.

- Read and study the Bible not just for knowledge, but also for wisdom.

- Read it as a story of redemption.

- Read it from a proper perspective.

- Use the Bible as words of life.

- Never be legalistic or dogmatic.

- Keep it simple: Love God and love people. I mean *really* love people.

Humility, kindness, and gentleness will produce more fruit than you can imagine. Pursue these virtues with all diligence. Never stop your pursuit!

Jesus said, "*Follow Me*" (Matthew 4:19 KJV). This precisely describes the organic Christian life. To know the Bible is a worthy goal. To know the Author of the Bible is life itself. Jesus is the Author and Finisher of our faith (Hebrews 12:2). To follow Jesus means that we do our best to know His heart, passion, thoughts, feelings, compassion, forgiveness, worldview, voice, and direction, to name a few. Finally, protect your new life as your personal garden. Keep it free from toxins. Keep it simple. Keep it organic!

Conclusion

CPSIA information can be obtained
at www.ICGtesting.com
Printed in the USA
BVHW051925140821
613930BV00008B/141